Table of Contents

Free Gift 6
Introduction 7
Vegan Slow Cooker Breakfast Recipes 8
    Delicious Oat Meal 8
    Breakfast Cherry Delight 8
    Crazy Maple and Pear Breakfast 9
    Hearty French Toast Bowls 9
    Tofu Burrito 10
    Tasty Mexican Breakfast 10
    Divine Carrot Oatmeal 11
    Wonderful Blueberry Butter 11
    Delicious Pumpkin Butter 12
    Delicious Breakfast Quinoa 12
    Apple Crumble 13
    Delicious Banana and Coconut Milk Delight 13
    Carrot and Zucchini Surprising Breakfast 14
    Simple Quinoa and Cranberries Breakfast 14
    Delicious Banana Bread 15
    Breakfast Energy Bars 15
    Tasty Breakfast Buns 16
    Cornbread Casserole 17
    Delicious Tapioca Pudding 17
    Incredible Rice Pudding 18
    Lentils Sandwich 18
    Breakfast Quinoa Pudding 19
    Simple Fruity Breakfast 19
    Wonderful Breakfast Idea 20
    Special Tea Breakfast 20
    Pumpkin Breakfast Delight 21
    Breakfast Fajitas 21
    Breakfast Enchiladas 22
    Delicious Coconut Porridge 22
    Rice Porridge 23
    Hearty Breakfast Casserole 23
    Slow Cooker Breakfast Oats 24
    Delicious Pear Oatmeal 24
    Cranberry French Toast 25
    Pumpkin Pecan Oatmeal 25
    Tasty Breakfast Burrito 26
    Healthy Steel Cut Oats 26
    Breakfast Tofu Casserole 27
    Carrot Oatmeal 27
    Delicious Vegan Scramble 28
    Blueberries Oatmeal 28
    Sweet Apple And Pears Breakfast 29
    Almond Butter Oatmeal 29
    Banana Oatmeal 30
    Delicious Vegan Frittata 30
    Apple Granola 31
    Carrot And Zucchini Oatmeal 31
    Cranberry Breakfast Quinoa 32
    Delicious Quinoa And Oats 32
    Breakfast Chia Pudding 33
Vegan Slow Cooker Side Dish Recipes 34

Collard Greens Delight 34
Mexican Black Beans 34
Amazing Carrots Surprise 35
Summer Black Eyed Peas 35
Flavored Beets 36
Great Beans and Lentils Dish 36
Easy Sweet Potatoes Dish 37
Wonderful Wild Rice 37
Delicious Mashed Potatoes 38
Delicious Barley and Squash Gratin 38
Beans, Carrots and Spinach Side Dish 39
Scalloped Potatoes.. 39
Sweet Potatoes Side Dish 40
Cauliflower And Broccoli Side Dish 40
Wild Rice Mix 41
Rustic Mashed Potatoes 41
Glazed Carrots 42
Mushroom And Peas Risotto 42
Squash And Spinach Mix 43
Chickpeas And Veggies 43
Eggplant And Kale Mix 44
Thai Veggie Mix 44
Simple Potatoes Side Dish 45
Brussels Sprouts 45
Beets And Carrots 46
Italian Veggie Side Dish 46
Acorn Squash And Great Sauce 47
Pilaf 47
Special Potatoes Mix 48
Creamy Corn 48
Vegan Slow Cooker Snack And Appetizer Recipes 49
Chipotle Tacos 49
Tasty Spinach Dip... 49
Candied Almonds 50
Eggplant Tapenade 50
Almond and Beans Fondue 51
Beans in Rich Tomato Sauce 51
Tasty Onion Dip 52
Special Beans Dip.. 52
Sweet and Spicy Nuts 53
Delicious Corn Dip 53
Butternut Squash Spread 54
Cashew And White Bean Spread 54
Vegan Rolls 55
Eggplant Appetizer 55
Vegan Veggie Dip 56
Great Bolognese Dip... 56
Black Eyed Peas Pate 57
Tofu Appetizer 57
Hummus... 58
Vegan Cashew Spread 58
Spinach Dip 59
Chowder 59
Appetizer Potato Salad 60
Veggie Appetizer... 60
Black Bean Appetizer Salad 61
Colored Stuffed Bell Peppers... 61

Corn Dip...62

Artichoke Spread..62

Mushroom Spread..63

Three Bean Dip...63

Vegan Slow Cooker Main Dish Recipes...64

Classic Black Beans Chili...64

Amazing Potato Dish..65

Textured Sweet Potatoes and Lentils Delight..65

Incredibly Tasty Pizza..66

Rich Beans Soup...66

Delicious Baked Beans...67

Indian Lentils..67

Delicious Butternut Squash Soup...68

Amazing Mushroom Stew..68

Simple Tofu Dish..69

Special Jambalaya...69

Delicious Chard Soup...70

Chinese Tofu and Veggies..70

Wonderful Corn Chowder..71

Black Eyed Peas Stew...71

White Bean Cassoulet...72

Light Jackfruit Dish..72

Veggie Curry...73

Chickpeas Soup..73

Hot and Delicious Soup..74

Delicious Eggplant Salad...74

Tasty Black Beans Soup..75

Rich Sweet Potato Soup...75

Pumpkin Chili...76

Crazy Cauliflower and Zucchini Surprise...76

Quinoa and Veggies..77

Spaghetti Squash Bowls...77

Amazing Curry..78

Lentils and Lemon Soup..78

Autumn Veggie Mix...79

Special Veggie Stew..79

Vegan Chickpeas Winter Mix...80

Indian Lentils Mix..80

"Baked" Beans...81

Squash Chili...81

Rich Lentils Soup..82

Easy Lentils Mix...82

Quinoa And Beans Chili...83

Potatoes And Spinach Mix...83

Rich White Bean Soup..84

Intense Tofu And Pineapple Mix..84

Vegan Jambalaya...85

Ratatouille...85

Pinto Beans And Tasty Rice...86

Black Beans, Rice And Mango...86

Spinach Soup...87

Split Pea Soup...87

Yam Stew...88

Special Minestrone Soup..88

Green Chili Soup...89

Caribbean Dish..89

Mediterranean Stew...90

Chickpeas Delight..90
Mexican Quinoa Dish...91
Sweet Potato Soup..91
White Beans Stew..92
Spaghetti Squash Bowls...92
Italian Cauliflower Mix..93
Mushroom Delight..93
Quinoa And Veggie Mix...94
Bulgur Chili..94
Cauliflower Chili..95
Quinoa Chili...95
Pumpkin Chili...96
3 Bean Chili..96
Root Vegetable Chili..97
Brown Rice Soup..97
Butternut Squash Soup...98
Green Beans Soup...98
Rich Chickpeas And Lentils Soup.......................................99
Chard And Sweet Potato Soup...99
Chinese Soup And Ginger Sauce.......................................100
Corn Cream Soup..100
Veggie Medley...101
Lentils Curry...101
Lentils Dal...102
Rich Jackfruit Dish...102
Vegan Gumbo..103
Eggplant Salad..103
Corn And Cabbage Soup..104
Okra Soup..104
Carrot Soup...105
Baby Carrots And Coconut Soup......................................105
Chinese Carrot Cream..106
Seitan Stew..106
Spicy Carrot Stew...107
Tomato Soup..107
Classic Tomato Soup..108
Collard Greens Mix..108
Colored Collard Greens Dish...109
Chinese Collard Greens Mix..109
Fresh Collard Greens Mix..110
Artichoke Soup...110
Intense Beet Soup...111
Brussels Sprouts Delight..111
Mushroom Soup..112
Beets And Capers Mix..112
Asparagus Soup..113
Fennel Soup...113
Endives Soup...114
Vegan Slow Cooker Dessert Recipes 115
Delicious Cake..115
Strawberry Cobbler..115
Spicy Pears..116
Delicious Apples...116
Fruit Compote...117
Pumpkin Pudding...117
Delicious Peanut Butter Cake 118
Tasty Apple Crisp...118

Delicious Peach Cake...119
Delicious Blueberry Pudding..119
Tasty Pear Delight 120
Easy Almond Pudding..120
Delicious Cinnamon Casserole...121
Strawberry Jam 121
Amazing Hot Fruits..122
Stewed Plums...122
Plums and Apples Surprise 123
Wonderful Plum Butter 123
Delicious Banana Dessert 124
Stewed Rhubarb 124
Pudding Cake...125
Sweet Peanut Butter Cake..125
Blueberry Cake 126
Peach Cobbler 126
Apple Mix 127
Pears And Dried Fruits Bowls..127
Strawberry Stew 128
Poached Plums 128
Bananas And Agave Sauce 129
Orange Cake...129
Stewed Apples 130
Pears And Orange Sauce 130
Almond Cookies 131
Pumpkin Cake..131
Strawberries Jam..132
Lemon Jam 132
Strawberries And Rhubarb Marmalade 133
Sweet Potatoes Pudding 133
Cherry Marmalade 134
Rice Pudding 134
Conclusion..135
Recipe Index...136

Free Gift

Up to 1000 delicious and healthy recipes from cooking traditions all around the world.

Please follow this link to get instant access to your Free Cookbook:
http://www.bookbuying.top/

Introduction

Do you sometimes feel that it's time for a change?
Are you wondering what can you do to live a healthier life from now on?
Don't you know?

We discovered the answer: you can become a vegan!
Don't get scared! Veganism is not so complex! It one of the most healthy lifestyles ever and once you discover what it means you will love it! You will soon recommend veganism to others!
Trust us!

So, what it veganism? Well, it's pretty simple! It's a way of life which excludes the consumption of all kind of animal ingredients or products.
Vegans don't consume meat, dairy products, eggs or honey but they consume veggies, fruits, legumes, grains and healthy replacements for animal-based products.
If you choose veganism as a way of life, you will be able to eat a lot of colored, rich and delicious meals. You won't even miss your old lifestyle!

If you've made the decision to try veganism, then we have another suggestion for you! We recommend you to try making your vegan meals using your slow cooker!
Yes, you've heard it right!
Slow cookers are the future in the kitchen and they help you cook healthier and easier!
So, why don't you combine this amazing lifestyle and the best kitchen appliance ever?

Are you ready to begin your culinary journey through vegan slow-cooked meals?
It will be the journey of a lifetime!
Enjoy!

Vegan Slow Cooker Breakfast Recipes

Delicious Oat Meal

Preparation time: 10 minutes
Cooking time: 6 hours
Servings: 4

Ingredients:

- 3 cups water
- 3 cups almond milk
- 1 and ½ cups steel oats
- 4 dates, pitted and chopped
- 1 teaspoon cinnamon, ground
- 2 tablespoons coconut sugar
- ½ teaspoon ginger powder
- A pinch of nutmeg, ground
- A pinch of cloves, ground
- 1 teaspoon vanilla extract

Directions:

1. Put water and milk in your slow cooker and stir.
2. Add oats, dates, cinnamon, sugar, ginger, nutmeg, cloves and vanilla extract, stir, cover and cook on Low for 6 hours.
3. Divide into bowls and serve for breakfast.

Enjoy!

Nutrition: calories 120, fat 1, fiber 2, carbs 3, protein 5

Breakfast Cherry Delight

Preparation time: 10 minutes
Cooking time: 8 hours and 10 minutes
Servings: 4

Ingredients:

- 2 cups almond milk
- 2 cups water
- 1 cup steel cut oats
- 2 tablespoons cocoa powder
- 1/3 cup cherries, pitted
- ¼ cup maple syrup
- ½ teaspoon almond extract

For the sauce:
- 2 tablespoons water
- 1 and ½ cups cherries, pitted and chopped
- ¼ teaspoon almond extract

Directions:

1. Put the almond milk in your slow cooker.
2. Add 2 cups water, oats, cocoa powder, 1/3 cup cherries, maples syrup and ½ teaspoon almond extract.
3. Stir, cover and cook on Low for 8 hours.
4. In a small pan, mix 2 tablespoons water with 1 and ½ cups cherries and ¼ teaspoon almond extract, stir well, bring to a simmer over medium heat and cook for 10 minutes until it thickens.
5. Divide oatmeal into breakfast bowls, top with the cherries sauce and serve.

Enjoy!

Nutrition: calories 150, fat 1, fiber 2, carbs 6, protein 5

Crazy Maple and Pear Breakfast

Preparation time: 10 minutes
Cooking time: 9 hours
Servings: 2

Ingredients:

- 1 pear, cored and chopped
- ½ teaspoon maple extract
- 2 cups coconut milk
- ½ cup steel cut oats
- ½ teaspoon vanilla extract
- 1 tablespoon stevia
- ¼ cup walnuts, chopped for serving
- Cooking spray

Directions:

1. Spray your slow cooker with some cooking spray and add coconut milk.
2. Also, add maple extract, oats, pear, stevia and vanilla extract, stir, cover and cook on Low for 9 hours.
3. Stir your oatmeal again, divide it into breakfast bowls and serve with chopped walnuts on top.

Enjoy!

Nutrition: calories 150, fat 3, fiber 2, carbs 6, protein 6

Hearty French Toast Bowls

Preparation time: 10 minutes
Cooking time: 5 hours
Servings: 4

Ingredients:

- 1 and ½ cups almond milk
- 1 cup coconut cream
- 1 tablespoon vanilla extract
- ½ tablespoon cinnamon powder
- 2 tablespoons maple syrup
- ¼ cup spenda
- 2 apples, cored and cubed
- ½ cup cranberries, dried
- 1 pound vegan bread, cubed
- Cooking spray

Directions:

1. Spray your slow cooker with some cooking spray and add the bread.
2. Also, add cranberries and apples and stir gently.
3. Add milk, coconut cream, maple syrup, vanilla extract, cinnamon powder and splenda.
4. Stir, cover and cook on Low for 5 hours.
5. Divide into bowls and serve right away.

Enjoy!

Nutrition: calories 140, fat 2, fiber 3, carbs 6, protein 2

Tofu Burrito

Preparation time: 10 minutes
Cooking time: 8 hours
Servings: 4

Ingredients:

- 15 ounces canned black beans, drained
- 2 tablespoons onions, chopped
- 7 ounces tofu, drained and crumbled
- 2 tablespoons green bell pepper, chopped
- ½ teaspoon turmeric
- ¾ cup water
- ¼ teaspoon smoked paprika
- ¼ teaspoon cumin, ground
- ¼ teaspoon chili powder
- A pinch of salt and black pepper
- 4 gluten free whole wheat tortillas
- Avocado, chopped for serving
- Salsa for serving

Directions:

1. Put black beans in your slow cooker.
2. Add onions, tofu, bell pepper, turmeric, water, paprika, cumin, chili powder, a pinch of salt and pepper, stir, cover and cook on Low for 8 hours.
3. Divide this on each tortilla, add avocado and salsa, wrap, arrange on plates and serve.

Enjoy!

Nutrition: calories 130, fat 4, fiber 2, carbs 5, protein 4

Tasty Mexican Breakfast

Preparation time: 10 minutes
Cooking time: 2 hours
Servings: 4

Ingredients:

- 1 cup brown rice
- 1 cup onion, chopped
- 2 cups veggie stock
- 1 red bell pepper, chopped
- 1 green bell pepper, chopped
- 4 ounces canned green chilies, chopped
- 15 ounces canned black beans, drained
- A pinch of salt
- Black pepper to the taste
-

For the salsa:
- 3 tablespoons lime juice
- 1 avocado, pitted, peeled and cubed
- ½ cup cilantro, chopped
- ½ cup green onions, chopped
- ½ cup tomato, chopped
- 1 poblano pepper, chopped
- 2 tablespoons olive oil
- ½ teaspoon cumin

Directions:

1. Put the stock in your slow cooker.
   Add rice, onions and beans, stir, cover and cook on High for 1 hour and 30 minutes.
2. Add chilies, red and green bell peppers, a pinch of salt and black pepper, stir, cover again and cook on High for 30 minutes more.
3. Meanwhile, in a bowl, mix avocado with green onions, tomato, poblano pepper, cilantro, oil, cumin, a pinch of salt, black pepper and lime juice and stir really well.
4. Divide rice mix into bowls; top each with the salsa you've just made and serve.

Nutrition: calories 140, fat 2, fiber 2, carbs 5, protein 5

Divine Carrot Oatmeal

Preparation time: 10 minutes
Cooking time: 7 hours
Servings: 3

Ingredients:

- 2 cups coconut milk
- ½ cup old fashioned rolled oats
- 1 cup carrots, chopped
- 2 tablespoons agave nectar
- 1 teaspoon cardamom, ground
- A pinch of saffron
- Some chopped pistachios
- Cooking spray

Directions:

1. Spray your slow cooker with some cooking spray and add coconut milk.
2. Also, add oats, carrots, agave nectar, cardamom and saffron.
3. Stir, cover and cook on Low for 7 hours.
4. Stir oatmeal again, divide into bowls and serve with chopped pistachios on top.

Enjoy!

Nutrition: calories 140, fat 2, fiber 2, carbs 4, protein 5

Wonderful Blueberry Butter

Preparation time: 10 minutes
Cooking time: 6 hours
Servings: 12

Ingredients:

- 5 cups blueberries puree
- 2 teaspoons cinnamon powder
- Zest from 1 lemon
- 1 cup coconut sugar
- ½ teaspoon nutmeg, ground
- ¼ teaspoon ginger, ground

Directions:

1. Put blueberries in your slow cooker, cover and cook on Low for 1 hour.
2. Stir your berries puree, cover and cook on Low for 4 hours more.
3. Add sugar, ginger, nutmeg and lemon zest, stir and cook on High uncovered for 1 hour more.
4. Divide into jars, cover them and keep in a cold place until you serve it for breakfast.

Enjoy!

Nutrition: calories 143, fat 2, fiber 3, carbs 3, protein 4

Delicious Pumpkin Butter

Preparation time: 10 minutes
Cooking time: 4 hours
Servings: 5

Ingredients:

- 2 teaspoons cinnamon powder
- 4 cups pumpkin puree
- 1 and ¼ cup maple syrup
- ½ teaspoon nutmeg
- 1 teaspoon vanilla extract

Directions:

1. In your slow cooker, mix pumpkin puree with maple syrup and vanilla extract, stir, cover and cook on High for 4 hours.
2. Add cinnamon and nutmeg, stir, divide into jars and serve for breakfast!

Enjoy!

Nutrition: calories 120, fat 2, fiber 2, carbs 4, protein 2

Delicious Breakfast Quinoa

Preparation time: 10 minutes
Cooking time: 8 hours
Servings: 4

Ingredients:

- 2 cups water
- 1 cup coconut milk
- 2 tablespoons maple syrup
- 1 cup quinoa, rinsed
- 1 teaspoon vanilla extract
- Berries for serving

Directions:

1. Put the water in your slow cooker.
2. Add milk, maple syrup and quinoa, stir, cover and cook on Low for 8 hours.
3. Fluff quinoa mix a bit, divide into bowls, add vanilla extract, stir and serve with your favorite berries on top.

Enjoy!

Nutrition: calories 120, fat 2, fiber 1, carbs 4, protein 4

Apple Crumble

Preparation time: 10 minutes
Cooking time: 4 hours
Servings: 4

Ingredients:

- 1 cup granola
- 2 apples, peeled, cored and cut into chunks
- 1/8 cup maple syrup
- 2 tablespoons coconut butter
- ¼ cup apple juice
- ½ teaspoon nutmeg, ground
- 1 teaspoon cinnamon, ground

Directions:

1. Put the apples in your slow cooker.
2. Add maple syrup, butter, apple juice, nutmeg and cinnamon.
3. Stir gently, sprinkle granola on top, cover and cook on Low for 4 hours.
4. Divide into bowls and serve.

Enjoy!

Nutrition: calories 160, fat 1, fiber 2, carbs 4, protein 5

Delicious Banana and Coconut Milk Delight

Preparation time: 10 minutes
Cooking time: 7 hours
Servings: 6

Ingredients:

- 2 cups bananas, peeled and sliced
- 28 ounces canned coconut milk
- 1 cup steel cut oats
- ½ cup water
- 2 tablespoons palm sugar
- 1 and ½ tablespoons coconut butter
- ¼ teaspoon nutmeg, ground
- ½ teaspoon cinnamon powder
- 1 tablespoon flax seed, ground
- ½ teaspoon vanilla extract
- A pinch of sea salt
- Chopped walnuts for serving
- Cooking spray

Directions:

1. Grease your slow cooker with cooking spray and add coconut milk.
2. Also, add bananas, oats, water, palm sugar, coconut butter, cinnamon, nutmeg, flax seed and a pinch of salt.
   Stir, cover and cook on Low for 7 hours.
   Divide into bowls and serve with chopped walnuts on top.

Enjoy!

Nutrition: calories 150, fat 2, fiber 1, carbs 5, protein 7

Carrot and Zucchini Surprising Breakfast

Preparation time: 10 minutes
Cooking time: 8 hours
Servings: 4

Ingredients:

- 1 and ½ cups almond milk
- ½ cup steel cut oats
- A pinch of nutmeg, ground
- 1 small zucchini, grated
- 1 carrot, grated
- A pinch of cloves, ground
- 2 tablespoons agave nectar
- ½ teaspoon cinnamon powder
- ¼ cup pecans, chopped

Directions:

1. Put the milk in your slow cooker and mix with oats, zucchini, carrots, nutmeg, cloves, cinnamon and agave nectar.
2. Stir, cover and cook on Low for 8 hours.
3. Add pecans, stir gently, divide into bowls and serve right away.

Enjoy!

Nutrition: calories 120, fat 1, fiber 2, carbs 5, protein 8

Simple Quinoa and Cranberries Breakfast

Preparation time: 10 minutes
Cooking time: 4 hours
Servings: 4

Ingredients:

- ¼ cup cranberries, dried
- 1/8 cup coconut flakes
- 1/8 cup almonds, sliced
- 3 teaspoons agave nectar
- 1 cup quinoa
- 3 cups water
- 1 teaspoon vanilla extract

Directions:

1. Put the water in your slow cooker.
2. Add quinoa, vanilla extract, cranberries, coconut flakes, agave nectar and almonds, stir, cover and cook on Low for 4 hours.
3. Fluff quinoa with a fork before dividing into bowls and serving.

Enjoy!

Nutrition: calories 120, fat 2, fiber 1, carbs 6, protein 7

Delicious Banana Bread

Preparation time: 10 minutes
Cooking time: 4 hours
Servings: 6

Ingredients:

- 3 bananas, peeled and mashed
- 1 teaspoon baking powder
- ½ teaspoon baking soda
- 2 cups whole wheat flour
- 1 cup palm sugar
- 2 tablespoons flax meal + 1 tablespoon water
- ½ cup coconut butter, melted

Directions:

1. In a bowl, mix sugar with flour, baking soda and baking powder and stir.
2. Add flax meal mixed with the water, butter and bananas, stir really well and pour the mix into a greased round pan that fits your slow cooker.
3. Arrange the pan into your slow cooker, cover and cook on Low for 4 hours.
4. Leave your bread to cool down, slice and serve it for breakfast.

Enjoy!

Nutrition: calories 160, fat 3, fiber 3, carbs 7, protein 6

Breakfast Energy Bars

Preparation time: 10 minutes
Cooking time: 4 hours
Servings: 8

Ingredients:

- ½ teaspoon cinnamon
- 1 cup almond milk
- 1/3 cup quinoa
- 2 tablespoons chia seeds
- 1/3 cup apple, dried and chopped
- ½ cup raisins
- 2 tablespoons maple syrup
- 2 tablespoons almond butter, melted
- 1/3 cup almonds, roasted and chopped
- 2 tablespoons flax meal + 1 tablespoon water
- Cooking spray

Directions:

1. Grease your slow cooker with cooking spray and add a parchment paper inside.
2. In a bowl, mix melted almond butter with maple syrup and whisk really well.
3. Add cinnamon and almond milk and whisk everything.
4. Add flax meal mixed with water and stir well again.
5. Transfer this to your slow cooker, add quinoa, chia, apples and raisins, stir really well and press into the slow cooker.
6. Cover and cook on Low for 4 hours.
7. Take quinoa sheet out of the slow cooker using the parchment paper as handles, leave aside to cool down, slice and serve.

Enjoy!

Nutrition: calories 140, fat 3, fiber 2, carbs 6, protein 5

Tasty Breakfast Buns

Preparation time: 10 minutes
Cooking time: 2 hours
Servings: 6
Ingredients:

- 6 tablespoons almond milk, hot
- ½ tablespoon coconut butter, melted
- 4 tablespoons maple syrup
- 1 teaspoon vanilla extract
- 2 and ¼ teaspoons yeast
- 2 cups whole wheat flour
- Cooking spray
  For the sauce:
- ¼ cup pecans, chopped
- 2 tablespoons almond milk
- 2 tablespoons coconut butter, melted
- 4 tablespoons maple syrup
  For the filling:
- ½ tablespoons coconut butter, melted
- 3 tablespoons maple syrup
- 1 and ½ teaspoons cinnamon powder

Directions:

1. In a bowl, mix 6 tablespoons milk with ½ tablespoon butter, 1 teaspoon vanilla extract and 4 tablespoons maple syrup, stir well and heat up in your microwave for a few seconds.
2. Add flour and yeast, knead really well until you obtain a dough and leave aside for now.
3. In a bowl, mix 2 tablespoons almond milk with 2 tablespoons coconut butter, 4 tablespoons maple syrup and pecans and stir really well.
4. In another bowl, mix ½ tablespoon coconut butter with 3 tablespoons maple syrup and cinnamon powder and stir well.
5. Divide your dough into 12 rectangles and brush each with the cinnamon filling.
6. Roll and shape 12 balls and dip each in the maple syrup and pecans sauce you've made.
7. Grease your slow cooker with the cooking spray and arrange your sweet buns in it.
8. Cover and cook on Low for 2 hours.
9. Leave your buns to cool down completely before serving.

Enjoy!

Nutrition: calories 200, fat 4, fiber 3, carbs 7, protein 5

Cornbread Casserole

Preparation time: 10 minutes
Cooking time: 2 hours and 30 minutes
Servings: 6
Ingredients:

- 3 garlic cloves, minced
- 1 green bell pepper, chopped
- 1 yellow onion, chopped
- 15 ounces canned black beans, drained
- 15 ounces canned red kidney beans, drained
- 15 ounces canned pinto beans, drained
- 15 ounces canned tomatoes, chopped
- 10 ounces tomato sauce
- 10 ounces canned corn, drained
- 2 teaspoons chili powder
- 1 teaspoon hot sauce
- A pinch of salt and pepper
- ½ cup yellow corn meal
- ½ cup almond flour
- 1 and ¼ teaspoons baking powder
- 1 tablespoon palm sugar
- ¾ cup almond milk
- 1 tablespoon chia seeds
- 1 and ½ tablespoons vegetable oil
- Cooking spray

Directions:

1. Heat up a pan over medium high heat, add garlic, bell pepper and onions, brown them for 7 minutes and transfer them to your slow cooker after you've sprayed with cooking spray.
2. Add black beans, pinto beans, red kidney beans, tomatoes, tomato sauce, corn, chili powder, salt, pepper and hot sauce, stir, cover and cook on High for 1 hour.
3. Meanwhile, in a bowl, mix almond flour with cornmeal, baking powder, sugar, milk, chia seeds and vegetable oil and stir really well.
4. Add this to the slow cooker and spread.
5. Cover slow cooker again and cook on High for 1 hour and 30 minutes more.
6. Leave your cornbread to cool down before slicing and serving.

Enjoy!

Nutrition: calories 240, fat 4, fiber 2, carbs 6, protein 9

Delicious Tapioca Pudding

Preparation time: 10 minutes
Cooking time: 2 hours
Servings: 6

Ingredients:

- 4 cups coconut milk
- ½ cup pearl tapioca
- 1 teaspoon vanilla extract
- 2 teaspoons orange extract

Directions:

1. Put coconut milk in your slow cooker.
2. Add tapioca, vanilla and orange extract, stir, cover and cook on High for 2 hours.
3. Divide into bowls and serve for breakfast.

Enjoy!

Nutrition: calories 140, fat 1, fiber 2, carbs 3, protein 5

Incredible Rice Pudding

Preparation time: 10 minutes
Cooking time: 3 hours
Servings: 2

Ingredients:

- ½ cup coconut sugar
- 2 cups almond milk
- ½ cup brown rice
- 1 teaspoon vanilla extract
- 1 tablespoons flax seed meal
- ½ cup raisins
- 1 teaspoon cinnamon powder

Directions:

1. Put the milk in your slow cooker.
2. Add rice and sugar and stir well.
3. Also, add flaxseed meal, raisins, vanilla and cinnamon, stir, cover and cook on Low for 2 hours.
4. Stir your pudding again, cover and cook on Low for 1 more hour.
5. Divide into bowls and serve.

Enjoy!

Nutrition: calories 160, fat 2, fiber 3, carbs 8, protein 12

Lentils Sandwich

Preparation time: 10 minutes
Cooking time: 1 hour and 30 minutes
Servings: 4

Ingredients:

- ½ cup blackstrap molasses
- 28 ounces canned tomatoes, crushed
- 6 ounces tomato paste
- ¼ cup white vinegar
- 2 tablespoons apple cider vinegar
- 1 sweet onion, chopped
- 3 garlic cloves, minced
- 1 teaspoon dry mustard
- 1 tablespoon coconut sugar
- ¼ teaspoon red pepper flakes
- A pinch of sea salt
- ¼ teaspoon liquid smoke
- A pinch of cayenne
- 4 cups green lentils, cooked and drained

Directions:

1. Put molasses in your slow cooker.
2. Add tomatoes, tomato paste, vinegar, apple cider vinegar, onion, garlic, mustard, sugar, salt, pepper flakes, cayenne and liquid smoke.
3. Stir everything, cover your slow cooker and cook on High for 1 hour and 30 minutes.
4. Add lentils, stir gently, divide on vegan buns and serve for breakfast.

Enjoy!

Nutrition: calories 150, fat 3, fiber 4, carbs 6, protein 7

Breakfast Quinoa Pudding

Preparation time: 10 minutes
Cooking time: 1 hour and 30 minutes
Servings: 2

Ingredients:

- ¼ cup maple syrup
- 3 cups almond milk
- 1 cup quinoa
- 2 tablespoons vanilla extract

Directions:

1. Put quinoa in your slow cooker.
2. Add maple syrup and almond milk and stir.
3. Also add vanilla extract, stir, cover and cook on High for 1 hour and 30 minutes.
4. Stir your pudding again, divide into bowls and serve.

Enjoy!

Nutrition: calories 140, fat 2, fiber 2, carbs 5, protein 5

Simple Fruity Breakfast

Preparation time: 10 minutes
Cooking time: 8 hours
Servings: 6

Ingredients:

- 1 cup apricots, dried and chopped
- ¾ cup red quinoa
- ¾ cup steel cut oats
- 2 tablespoons agave nectar
- ½ teaspoon vanilla bean paste
- ¾ cup hazelnuts, toasted and chopped
- 6 cups water
- Chopped hazelnuts for serving

Directions:

1. In a bowl, mix quinoa with oats, vanilla bean paste, apricots, hazelnuts, agave nectar and water and stir well.
2. Pour this into your slow cooker, cover and cook on Low for 8 hours.
3. Stir again everything, divide into bowls and serve with more chopped hazelnuts on top.

Enjoy!

Nutrition: calories 251, fat 4, fiber 4, carbs 10, protein 7

Wonderful Breakfast Idea

Preparation time: 10 minutes
Cooking time: 2 hours
Servings: 4

Ingredients:

- 3 cups almond milk
- 1 cup quinoa
- 1 apple, cored, peeled and chopped
- ¼ cup pepitas
- 4 dates, chopped
- ¼ teaspoon nutmeg, ground
- 2 teaspoons cinnamon powder
- 1 teaspoon vanilla extract

Directions:

1. Put the milk in your slow cooker.
2. Add quinoa, apple, dates, pepitas, cinnamon, nutmeg and vanilla.
3. Stir, cover and cook on High for 2 hours.
4. Divide into bowls and serve for breakfast.

Enjoy!

Nutrition: calories 130, fat 3, fiber 6, carbs 10, protein 5

Special Tea Breakfast

Preparation time: 10 minutes
Cooking time: 6 hours
Servings: 4

Ingredients:

- ½ cup steel cut oats
- 2 cups brewed earl gray tea
- 2 tablespoons agave nectar
- ½ teaspoon rose water

Directions:

1. Put oats in your slow cooker.
2. Add tea, agave nectar and rose water, stir, cover and cook on Low for 6 hours.
3. Divide into bowls and serve for breakfast.

Enjoy!

Nutrition: calories 120, fat 2, fiber 3, carbs 5, protein 7

Pumpkin Breakfast Delight

Preparation time: 10 minutes
Cooking time: 6 hours
Servings: 4

Ingredients:

- 4 and ½ cups water
- 1 and ½ cups pumpkin puree
- 1 and ½ cups steel cut oats
- 1 teaspoon allspice
- 2 teaspoons cinnamon
- 1 teaspoon vanilla extract
- ½ cup coconut sugar
- ¼ cup pecans, chopped
- 1 tablespoon cinnamon powder

Directions:

1. In your slow cooker, mix water with pumpkin puree, oats, allspice, cinnamon and vanilla extract.
2. Stir, cover and cook on Low for 6 hours.
3. In a bowl, mix cinnamon with coconut sugar and pecans and stir.
4. Divide oats into bowls, sprinkle pecans mix on top and serve.

Enjoy!

Nutrition: calories 140, fat 3, fiber 2, carbs 7, protein 6

Breakfast Fajitas

Preparation time: 10 minutes
Cooking time: 2 hours
Servings: 8

Ingredients:

- 4 ounces canned green chilies, chopped
- 3 tomatoes, chopped
- 1 green bell pepper, chopped
- 1 yellow onion, chopped
- 1 red bell pepper, chopped
- 2 teaspoons cumin, ground
- ½ teaspoon oregano, dried
- 2 teaspoons chili powder
- A pinch of sea salt
- Black pepper to the taste
- 8 whole wheat tortillas
- 2 avocados, pitted, peeled and chopped
- Cooking spray

Directions:

1. Grease your slow cooker with some cooking spray and add chilies.
2. Also, add tomatoes, bell peppers, onion, cumin, oregano, chili powder, a pinch of salt and pepper, stir, cover and cook on High for 2 hours.
3. Stir again, divide veggies on tortillas, add avocado on top, wrap and serve for breakfast.

Enjoy!

Nutrition: calories 140, fat 3, fiber 2, carbs 8, protein 12

Breakfast Enchiladas

Preparation time: 10 minutes
Cooking time: 3 hours
Servings: 4

Ingredients:

- 10 ounces spinach
- 16 ounces canned black beans, drained
- 1 cup corn
- 2 cups cashew cheese, shredded
- ½ teaspoon cumin, ground
- A pinch of sea salt
- Black pepper to the taste
- 3 and ½ cups vegan salsa
- 4 corn tortillas
- 4 radishes, chopped
- 6 cups lettuce leaves, torn
- 1 small cucumber, chopped
- 1 small tomato, chopped
- 3 tablespoons lime juice
- 2 tablespoons olive oil

Directions:

1. Spread half of the salsa in your slow cooker.
2. Add beans, corn, spinach, cumin, half of the cashew cheese, salt and pepper and stir.
3. Top with the rest of the salsa and the rest of the cashew cheese, cover and cook on Low for 3 hours.
4. Divide this mix on warm corn tortillas, wrap and divide between plates.
5. In a bowl, mix cucumber with radishes, tomatoes, lettuce, lime juice and olive oil and toss to coat.
6. Serve enchiladas with cucumber and tomatoes mix on the side.

Enjoy!

Nutrition: calories 160, fat 3, fiber 4, carbs 10, protein 6

Delicious Coconut Porridge

Preparation time: 10 minutes
Cooking time: 7 hours
Servings: 4

Ingredients:

- 4 ounces jumbo rolled oats
- 13 ounces canned coconut milk
- ¼ teaspoon cinnamon powder
- 1 teaspoon coconut oil
- 7 ounces canned mango and pineapple chunks

Directions:

1. Put the milk in your slow cooker.
2. Add oats and cinnamon, stir, cover and cook on Low for 7 hours.
3. Stir your porridge and divide into bowls.
4. Heat up a pan with the oil over medium high heat, add mango and pineapple pieces, stir for about 1 minute and divide this on top of your porridge bowls.

Enjoy!

Nutrition: calories 240, fat 3, fiber 3, carbs 8, protein 10

Rice Porridge

Preparation time: 10 minutes
Cooking time: 8 hours
Servings: 6

Ingredients:

- 1 apple, cored and cubed
- 6 cups water
- 1 cup brown rice
- ½ cup coconut ,shredded
- 1/8 cup raisins
- ¼ teaspoon cinnamon powder
- ½ teaspoon pumpkin pie spice
- 1 tablespoon peanut butter
- Stevia to the taste

Directions:

1. Put the water in your slow cooker.
2. Add rice, apple, coconut, raisins, cinnamon and pumpkin pie spice.
3. Stir, cover and cook on low for 8 hours.
4. Stir your porridge, divide it into bowls and top with peanut butter and stevia.
5. Stir your porridge again before serving.

Enjoy!

Nutrition: calories 245, fat 4, fiber 3, carbs 7, protein 10

Hearty Breakfast Casserole

Preparation time: 10 minutes
Cooking time: 4 hours
Servings: 4

Ingredients:

- 2 teaspoons onion powder
- ¾ cup cashews, soaked for 30 minutes and drained
- ¼ cup nutritional yeast
- 1 teaspoon garlic powder
- ½ teaspoon sage, dried
- Salt and black pepper to the taste
- 1 yellow onion, chopped
- 2 tablespoons parsley, chopped
- 3 garlic cloves, minced
- 1 tablespoon olive oil
- 4 red potatoes, cubed
- ½ teaspoon red pepper flakes

Directions:

1. In your blender, mix cashews with onion powder, garlic powder, nutritional yeast, sage, salt and pepper and pulse really well.
2. Add oil to your slow cooker.
3. Arrange potatoes, pepper flakes, garlic, onion, salt, pepper and parsley and toss well.
4. Add cashews sauce, toss, cover and cook on High for 4 hours.
5. Arrange on plates and serve for breakfast.

Enjoy!

Nutrition: calories 218, fat 6, fiber 6, carbs 14, protein 5

Slow Cooker Breakfast Oats

Preparation time: 10 minutes
Cooking time: 8 hours and 10 minutes
Servings: 4

Ingredients:
- 2 cups almond milk
- 1 cup steel cut oats
- 2 cups water
- 1/3 cup cherries, dried
- 2 tablespoons cocoa powder
- ¼ cup stevia
- ½ teaspoon almond extract

For the sauce:
- 2 tablespoons water
- 1 and ½ cups cherries
- ¼ teaspoon almond extract

Directions:
1. In your slow cooker, mix almond milk with oats, water, dried cherries, cocoa powder, stevia and ½ teaspoon almond extract, stir, cover and cook on Low for 8 hours.
2. Meanwhile, in a small pot, mix 2 tablespoons water with 1 and ½ cups cherries and ¼ teaspoon almond extract, stir, bring to a simmer over medium heat and cook for 10 minutes.
3. Divide oats into bowls, drizzle cherry sauce all over and serve.

Enjoy!

Nutrition: calories 172, fat 7, fiber 7, carbs 12, protein 6

Delicious Pear Oatmeal

Preparation time: 10 minutes
Cooking time: 7 hours
Servings: 3

Ingredients:
- 2 cups coconut milk
- ½ cup steel cut oats
- ½ teaspoon vanilla extract
- 1 pear, chopped
- ½ teaspoon maple extract
- 1 tablespoon stevia

Directions:
1. In your slow cooker, mix coconut milk with oats, vanilla, pear, maple extract and stevia, stir, cover and cook on Low for 7 hours.
2. Divide into bowls and serve for breakfast.

Enjoy!

Nutrition: calories 200, fat 5, fiber 7, carbs 14, protein 4

Cranberry French Toast

Preparation time: 10 minutes
Cooking time: 5 hours
Servings: 4

Ingredients:

- 1 tablespoon chia seeds
- ½ tablespoon agave nectar
- 1 cup almond milk
- ½ teaspoon vanilla extract
- ½ teaspoon cinnamon powder
- 4 vegan bread slices, cubed
- 1 tablespoon coconut oil

Directions:

1. Add coconut oil to your slow cooker, also add bread cubes and toss a bit.
2. Also add milk, agave nectar, chia seeds, vanilla extract and cinnamon, toss, cover and cook on Low for 5 hours.
3. Divide into bowls and serve for breakfast.

Enjoy!

Nutrition: calories 231, fat 4, fiber 7, carbs 14, protein 4

Pumpkin Pecan Oatmeal

Preparation time: 10 minutes
Cooking time: 8 hours
Servings: 4

Ingredients:

- 1 and ½ cups water
- ½ cup pumpkin puree
- 1 teaspoon pumpkin pie spice
- 3 tablespoons stevia
- ½ cup steel cut oats
- ¼ cup pecans, chopped

Directions:

1. In your slow cooker mix water with oats, pumpkin puree, pumpkin spice and stevia, stir, cover and cook on Low for 8 hours.
2. Sprinkle pecans on top, toss, divide into bowls and serve for breakfast.

Enjoy!

Nutrition: calories 211, fat 4, fiber 7, carbs 8, protein 3

Tasty Breakfast Burrito

Preparation time: 10 minutes
Cooking time: 6 hours
Servings: 8

Ingredients:
- 16 ounces tofu, crumbled
- 1 green bell pepper, chopped
- ¼ cup scallions, chopped
- 15 ounces canned black beans, drained
- 1 cup vegan salsa
- ½ cup water
- ¼ teaspoon cumin, ground
- ½ teaspoon turmeric powder
- ½ teaspoon smoked paprika
- A pinch of salt and black pepper
- ¼ teaspoon chili powder
- 3 cups spinach leaves, torn
- 8 vegan tortillas for serving

Directions:
1. In your slow cooker, mix tofu with bell pepper, scallions, black beans, salsa, water, cumin, turmeric, paprika, salt, pepper and chili powder, stir, cover and cook on Low for 6 hours.
2. Add spinach, toss well, divide this on your vegan tortillas, roll, wrap them and serve for breakfast.

Enjoy!

Nutrition: calories 211, fat 4, fiber 7, carbs 14, protein 4

Healthy Steel Cut Oats

Preparation time: 10 minutes
Cooking time: 4 hours
Servings: 6

Ingredients:
- 1 and ½ cups water
- 1 and ½ cups coconut milk
- 2 apples, cored, peeled and chopped
- 1 cup steel cut oats
- ½ teaspoon cinnamon powder
- ¼ teaspoon nutmeg, ground
- ¼ teaspoon allspice, ground
- ¼ teaspoon ginger powder
- ¼ teaspoon cardamom, ground
- 1 tablespoon flax seed, ground
- 2 teaspoons vanilla extract
- 2 teaspoons stevia
- Cooking spray

Directions:
1. Spray your slow cooker with cooking spray, add apple pieces, milk, water, cinnamon, oats, allspice, nutmeg, cardamom, ginger, vanilla, flax seeds and stevia, stir, cover and cook on Low for 4 hours.
2. Stir oatmeal again, divide into bowls and serve.

Enjoy!

Nutrition: calories 162, fat 3, fiber 7, carbs 8, protein 5

Breakfast Tofu Casserole

Preparation time: 10 minutes
Cooking time: 4 hours
Servings: 4

Ingredients:
- 1 teaspoon lemon zest, grated
- 14 ounces tofu, cubed
- 1 tablespoon lemon juice
- 2 tablespoons nutritional yeast
- 1 tablespoon apple cider vinegar
- 1 tablespoon olive oil
- 2 garlic cloves, minced
- 10 ounces spinach, torn
- ½ cup yellow onion, chopped
- ½ teaspoon basil, dried
- 8 ounces mushrooms, sliced
- Salt and black pepper to the taste
- ¼ teaspoon red pepper flakes
- Cooking spray

Directions:
1. Spray your slow cooker with some cooking spray and arrange tofu cubes on the bottom.
2. Add lemon zest, lemon juice, yeast, vinegar, olive oil, garlic, spinach, onion, basil, mushrooms, salt, pepper and pepper flakes, toss, cover and cook on Low for 4 hours.
3. Divide between plates and serve for breakfast.

Enjoy!

Nutrition: calories 216, fat 6, fiber 8, carbs 12, protein 4

Carrot Oatmeal

Preparation time: 10 minutes
Cooking time: 7 hours
Servings: 4

Ingredients:
- 2 cups coconut milk
- ½ cup steel cut oats
- 1 cup carrots, shredded
- 1 teaspoon cardamom, ground
- ½ teaspoon agave nectar
- A pinch of saffron
- Cooking spray

Directions:
1. Spray your slow cooker with cooking spray, add milk, oats, carrots, cardamom and agave nectar, stir, cover and cook on Low for 7 hours.
2. Stir oatmeal again, divide into bowls, sprinkle saffron on top and serve for breakfast.

Enjoy!

Nutrition: calories 182, fat 7, fiber 4, carbs 8, protein 3

Delicious Vegan Scramble

Preparation time: 10 minutes
Cooking time: 8 hours
Servings: 4

Ingredients:
- 1 pound tofu, crumbled
- 1 pound white mushrooms, sliced
- 1 cup green onions, chopped
- 1 cup corn
- 1 tablespoon olive oil
- A pinch of salt and black pepper
- 1 zucchini, chopped
- ¼ cup coconut aminos
- ½ cup nutritional yeast
- 3 pounds baby red potatoes, halved

Directions:
1. In your slow cooker, mix oil with tofu, mushrooms, green onions, corn, salt, pepper, zucchini, aminos, yeast and potatoes, toss, cover and cook on Low for 8 hours.
2. Divide between plates and serve for breakfast.

Enjoy!

Nutrition: calories 222, fat 5, fiber 8, carbs 12, protein 4

Blueberries Oatmeal

Preparation time: 10 minutes
Cooking time: 8 hours
Servings: 4

Ingredients:
- 1 cup blueberries
- 1 cup steel cut oats
- 1 cup coconut milk
- 2 tablespoons agave nectar
- ½ teaspoon vanilla extract
- Coconut flakes for serving
- Cooking spray

Directions:
1. Spray your slow cooker with cooking spray, add oats, milk, agave nectar, vanilla and blueberries, toss, cover and cook on Low for 8 hours.
2. Stir your oatmeal one more time, divide into bowls, sprinkle coconut flakes all over and serve.

Enjoy!

Nutrition: calories 182, fat 6, fiber 8, carbs 9, protein 6

Sweet Apple And Pears Breakfast

Preparation time: 10 minutes
Cooking time: 6 hours
Servings: 6

Ingredients:
- 4 apples, cored, peeled and cut into medium chunks
- 1 teaspoon lemon juice
- 4 pears, cored, peeled and cut into medium chunks
- 5 teaspoons stevia
- 1 teaspoon cinnamon powder
- 1 teaspoon vanilla extract
- ½ teaspoon ginger, ground
- ½ teaspoon cloves, ground
- ½ teaspoon cardamom, ground

Directions:
1. In your slow cooker, mix apples with pears, lemon juice, stevia, cinnamon, vanilla extract, ginger, cloves and cardamom, stir, cover and cook on Low for 6 hours.
2. Divide into bowls and serve for breakfast.

Enjoy!

Nutrition: calories 201, fat 3, fiber 7, carbs 19, protein 4

Almond Butter Oatmeal

Preparation time: 10 minutes
Cooking time: 10 hours
Servings: 2

Ingredients:
- ½ cup steel cut oats
- ½ cup almond milk
- Seeds from 1 vanilla bean
- 1 cup water
- 4 tablespoons almond butter
- Stevia to the taste

Directions:
1. In 2 heatproof containers, divide oats, almond milk, vanilla seeds, water, stevia and almond butter and stir.
2. Arrange containers in your slow cooker, fill slow cooker halfway with water, cover and cook on Low for 10 hours.
3. Serve warm for breakfast.

Enjoy!

Nutrition: calories 182, fat 3, fiber 7, carbs 18, protein 4

Banana Oatmeal

Preparation time: 10 minutes
Cooking time: 8 hours
Servings: 4

Ingredients:
- 1 banana, peeled and mashed
- 1 cup steel cut oats
- 2 cups almond milk
- 2 cups water
- ¼ cup walnuts, chopped
- 2 tablespoons flax seed meal
- 2 teaspoons cinnamon powder
- 1 teaspoon vanilla extract
- ½ teaspoon nutmeg, ground

Directions:
1. In your slow cooker mix oats with almond milk, water, walnuts, flaxseed meal, cinnamon, vanilla and nutmeg, stir, cover and cook on Low for 8 hours.
2. Stir oatmeal one more time, divide into bowls and serve for breakfast.

Enjoy!

Nutrition: calories 291, fat 7, fiber 6, carbs 42, protein 11

Delicious Vegan Frittata

Preparation time: 10 minutes
Cooking time: 6 hours
Servings: 4

Ingredients:
- 1 pound firm tofu, drained, pressed and crumbled
- 2 tablespoons olive oil
- ¼ cup nutritional yeast
- 1 yellow onion, chopped
- ¼ teaspoon turmeric powder
- 3 tablespoons garlic, minced
- 1 red bell pepper, chopped
- ½ cup kalamata olives, pitted and halved
- 1 teaspoon basil, dried
- 1 teaspoon oregano, dried
- 1 tablespoon lemon juice
- Salt and black pepper to the taste

Directions:
1. Add the oil to your slow cooker and arrange crumbled tofu on the bottom.
2. Add yeast, onion, turmeric, garlic, bell pepper, olives, basil, oregano, lemon juice, salt and pepper, toss a bit, cover and cook on Low for 6 hours.
3. Divide frittata between plates and serve for breakfast.

Enjoy!

Nutrition: calories 271, fat 4, fiber 7, carbs 20, protein 6

Apple Granola

Preparation time: 10 minutes
Cooking time: 4 hours
Servings: 3

Ingredients:
- ½ cup granola
- ½ cup bran flakes
- 2 green apples, cored, peeled and roughly chopped
- ¼ cup apple juice
- 1/8 cup maple syrup
- 2 tablespoons cashew butter
- 1 teaspoon cinnamon powder
- ½ teaspoon nutmeg, ground

Directions:
1. In your slow cooker, mix granola with bran flakes, apples, apple juice, maple syrup, cashew butter, cinnamon and nutmeg, toss, cover and cook on Low for 4 hours.
2. Divide apple granola into bowls and serve for breakfast.

Enjoy!

Nutrition: calories 218, fat 6, fiber 9, carbs 17, protein 6

Carrot And Zucchini Oatmeal

Preparation time: 10 minutes
Cooking time: 8 hours
Servings: 4

Ingredients:
- ½ cup steel cut oats
- 1 carrot, grated
- 1 and ½ cups almond milk
- ¼ zucchini, grated
- A pinch of nutmeg, ground
- A pinch of cloves, ground
- ½ teaspoon cinnamon powder
- 2 tablespoons maple syrup
- ¼ cup pecans, chopped
- 1 teaspoon vanilla extract

Directions:
1. In your slow cooker, mix oats with carrot, zucchini, almond milk, cloves, nutmeg, cinnamon, maple syrup, pecans and vanilla extract, stir, cover and cook on Low for 8 hours.
2. Stir your oatmeal one more time, divide into bowls and serve.

Enjoy!

Nutrition: calories 215, fat 4, fiber 7, carbs 12, protein 7

Cranberry Breakfast Quinoa

Preparation time: 10 minutes
Cooking time: 2 hours
Servings: 4

Ingredients:
- 1 cup quinoa
- 3 cups coconut water
- 1 teaspoon vanilla extract
- 3 teaspoons stevia
- 1/8 cup coconut flakes
- ¼ cup cranberries, dried
- 1/8 cup almonds, chopped

Directions:
1. In your slow cooker, mix quinoa with coconut water, vanilla, stevia, coconut flakes, almonds and cranberries, toss, cover and cook on High for 2 hours.
2. Stir quinoa mix one more time, divide into bowls and serve for breakfast.

Enjoy!

Nutrition: calories 246, fat 5, fiber 5, carbs 30, protein 7

Delicious Quinoa And Oats

Preparation time: 10 minutes
Cooking time: 7 hours
Servings: 6

Ingredients:
- ½ cup quinoa
- 1 and ½ cups steel cut oats
- 4 tablespoons stevia
- 4 and ½ cups almond milk
- 2 tablespoons maple syrup
- 1 and ½ teaspoons vanilla extract
- Strawberries, halved for serving
- Cooking spray

Directions:
1. Spray your slow cooker with cooking spray, add oats, quinoa, stevia, almond milk, maple syrup and vanilla extract, toss, cover and cook on Low for 7 hours.
2. Divide into bowls, add strawberries on top and serve for breakfast.

Enjoy!

Nutrition: calories 267, fat 5, fiber 8, carbs 28, protein 5

Breakfast Chia Pudding

Preparation time: 10 minutes
Cooking time: 2 hours
Servings: 4

Ingredients:
- ½ cup coconut chia granola
- ½ cup chia seeds
- 2 cups coconut milk
- 2 tablespoons coconut, shredded and unsweetened
- ¼ cup maple syrup
- ½ teaspoon cinnamon powder
- 2 teaspoons cocoa powder
- ½ teaspoon vanilla extract

Directions:
1. In your slow cooker, mix chia granola with chia seeds, coconut milk, coconut, maple syrup, cinnamon, cocoa powder and vanilla, toss, cover and cook on High for 2 hours.
2. Divide chia pudding into bowls and serve for breakfast.

Enjoy!

Nutrition: calories 261, fat 4, fiber 8, carbs 10, protein 4

Vegan Slow Cooker Side Dish Recipes

Collard Greens Delight

Preparation time: 10 minutes
Cooking time: 4 hours and 5 minutes
Servings: 4

Ingredients:

- 1 tablespoons olive oil
- 1 cup yellow onion, chopped
- 16 ounces collard greens
- 2 garlic cloves, minced
- A pinch of sea salt
- Black pepper to the taste
- 14 ounces veggie stock
- 1 bay leaf
- 1 tablespoon agave nectar
- 3 tablespoon balsamic vinegar

Directions:

1. Heat up a pan with the oil over medium high heat, add onion, stir and cook for 3 minutes. Add collard greens, stir, cook for 2 minutes more and transfer to your slow cooker.
2. Add garlic, salt, pepper, stock and bay leaf, stir, cover and cook on Low for 4 hours.
3. In a bowl, mix vinegar with agave nectar and whisk well.
4. Add this to collard greens, stir, divide between plates and serve.

Enjoy!

Nutrition: calories 130, fat 1, fiber 2, carbs 5, protein 3

Mexican Black Beans

Preparation time: 10 minutes
Cooking time: 10 hours
Servings: 4

Ingredients:

- 1 pound black beans, soaked overnight and drained
- A pinch of sea salt
- Black pepper to the taste
- 3 cups veggie stock
- 2 cups yellow onion, chopped
- 1 tablespoon canned chipotle chili pepper in adobo sauce
- 4 garlic cloves, minced
- 1 tablespoon lime juice
- ½ cup cilantro, chopped
- ½ cup pumpkin seeds

Directions:

1. Put the beans in your slow cooker.
2. Add a pinch of salt, black pepper, onion, stock, garlic and chipotle chili in adobo sauce.
3. Stir, cover and cook on Low for 10 hours.
4. Add lime juice and mash beans a bit using a potato masher.
5. Add cilantro, stir gently, divide between plates and serve with pumpkin seeds on top.

Enjoy!

Nutrition: calories 150, fat 3, fiber 4, carbs 7, protein 5

Amazing Carrots Surprise

Preparation time: 10 minutes
Cooking time: 8 hours
Servings: 12

Ingredients:

- 3 pounds carrots, peeled and cut into medium pieces
- A pinch of sea salt
- Black pepper to the taste
- 2 tablespoons water
- ½ cup agave nectar
- 2 tablespoons olive oil
- ½ teaspoon orange rind, grated

Directions:

1. Put the oil in your slow cooker and add the carrots.
2. In a bowl mix agave nectar with water and whisk well.
3. Add this to your slow cooker as well.
4. Also, add a pinch of sea salt and black pepper, stir gently everything, cover and cook on Low for 8 hours.
5. Sprinkle orange rind all over, stir gently, divide on plates and serve.

Enjoy!

Nutrition: calories 140, fat 2, fiber 2, carbs 4, protein 6

Summer Black Eyed Peas

Preparation time: 10 minutes
Cooking time: 8 hours
Servings: 6

Ingredients:

- 3 cups black eyed peas
- A pinch of salt
- Black pepper to the taste
- 2 cups veggie stock
- 2 tablespoons jalapeno peppers, chopped
- 2 cups sweet onion, chopped
- ½ teaspoon thyme, dried
- 4 garlic cloves, minced
- 1 bay leaf
- Hot sauce to the taste

Directions:

1. Put the peas in your slow cooker.
2. Add a pinch of salt, black pepper, stock, jalapenos, onion, garlic, thyme and bay leaf.
3. Stir everything, cover and cook on Low for 8 hours.
4. Drizzle hot sauce over peas, stir gently, divide between plates and serve.

Enjoy!

Nutrition: calories 130, fat 2, fiber 4, carbs 7, protein 7

Flavored Beets

Preparation time: 10 minutes
Cooking time: 8 hours
Servings: 6

Ingredients:

- 6 beets, peeled and cut into wedges
- A pinch of sea salt
- Black pepper to the taste
- 2 tablespoons lemon juice
- 2 tablespoons olive oil
- 2 tablespoons agave nectar
- 1 tablespoon cider vinegar
- ½ teaspoon lemon rind, grated
- 2 rosemary sprigs

Directions:

1. Put the beets in your slow cooker.
2. Add a pinch of salt, black pepper, lemon juice, oil, agave nectar, rosemary and vinegar. Stir everything, cover and cook on Low for 8 hours.
3. Add lemon rind, stir, divide between plates and serve.

Enjoy!

Nutrition: calories 120, fat 1, fiber 2, carbs 6, protein 6

Great Beans and Lentils Dish

Preparation time: 10 minutes
Cooking time: 7 hours and 10 minutes
Servings: 6

Ingredients:

- 2 tablespoons thyme, chopped
- 1 tablespoon olive oil
- 1 cup yellow onion, chopped
- 5 cups water
- 5 garlic cloves, minced
- 3 tablespoons cider vinegar
- ½ cup tomato paste
- ½ cup maple syrup
- 3 tablespoons soy sauce
- 2 tablespoons Korean red chili paste
- 2 tablespoons dry mustard
- 1 and ½ cups great northern beans
- ½ cup red lentils

Directions:

1. Heat up a pan with the oil over medium high heat, add onion, stir and cook for 4 minutes.
2. Add garlic, thyme, vinegar and tomato paste, stir, cook for 5 minutes more and transfer to your slow cooker.
3. Add lentils and beans to your slow cooker and stir.
4. Also add water, maple syrup, mustard, chili paste and soy sauce, stir, cover and cook on High for 7 hours.
5. Stir beans mix again, divide between plates and serve.

Enjoy!

Nutrition: calories 160, fat 2, fiber 4, carbs 7, protein 8

Easy Sweet Potatoes Dish

Preparation time: 10 minutes
Cooking time: 6 hours
Servings: 6

Ingredients:

- 4 pounds sweet potatoes, peeled and sliced
- ½ cup orange juice
- 3 tablespoons palm sugar
- ½ teaspoon thyme, dried
- A pinch of sea salt
- Black pepper to the taste
- ½ teaspoon sage, dried
- 2 tablespoons olive oil

Directions:

1. Put the oil in your slow cooker and add sweet potato slices.
2. In a bowl, mix orange juice with palm sugar, thyme, sage, a pinch of salt and black pepper and whisk well.
   Add this over potatoes, toss to coat, cover slow cooker and cook on Low for 6 hours.
3. Stir sweet potatoes mix again, divide between plates and serve.

Enjoy!

Nutrition: calories 160, fat 3, fiber 2, carbs 6, protein 9

Wonderful Wild Rice

Preparation time: 10 minutes
Cooking time: 6 hours
Servings: 12

Ingredients:

- 42 ounces veggie stock
- 1 cup carrot, shredded
- 2 and ½ cups wild rice
- 4 ounces mushrooms, sliced
- 2 tablespoons olive oil
- 2 teaspoons marjoram, dried
- A pinch of sea salt
- Black pepper to the taste
- 2/3 cup cherries, dried
- ½ cup pecans, chopped
- 2/3 cup green onions, chopped

Directions:

1. Put the stock in your slow cooker.
2. Add rice, carrots, mushrooms, oil, salt, pepper marjoram.
3. Stir, cover and cook on Low for 6 hours.
4. Add cherries and green onions, stir, cover slow cooker and leave it aside for 10 minutes.
5. Divide wild rice between plates and serve with chopped pecans on top.

Enjoy!

Nutrition: calories 140, fat 2, fiber 3, carbs 6, protein 7

Delicious Mashed Potatoes

Preparation time: 10 minutes
Cooking time: 6 hours
Servings: 12

Ingredients:

- 3 pounds russet potatoes, peeled and cubed
- 6 garlic cloves, chopped
- 28 ounces veggie stock
- 1 bay leaf
- 1 cup coconut milk
- ¼ cup coconut butter
- A pinch of sea salt
- White pepper to the taste

Directions:

1. Put potatoes in your slow cooker.
2. Add stock, garlic and bay leaf, stir, cover and cook on Low for 6 hours.
3. Drain potatoes, discard bay leaf, return them to your slow cooker and mash using a potato masher.
4. Meanwhile, put the coconut milk in a pot, stir and heat up over medium heat.
5. Add coconut butter and stir until it dissolves.
6. Add this to your mashed potatoes, season with a pinch of salt and white pepper, stir well, divide between plates and serve as a side dish.

Enjoy!

Nutrition: calories 1535, fat 4, fiber 2, carbs 10, protein 4

Delicious Barley and Squash Gratin

Preparation time: 10 minutes
Cooking time: 7 hours
Servings: 12

Ingredients:

- 2 pounds butternut squash, peeled and cubed
- 1 yellow onion, cut into medium wedges
- 10 ounces spinach
- 1 cup barley
- 14 ounces veggie stock
- ½ cup water
- A pinch of salt
- Black pepper to the taste
- 3 garlic cloves, minced

Directions:

1. Put squash pieces in your slow cooker.
2. Add barley, spinach, stock, water, onion, garlic, salt and pepper, stir, cover and cook on Low for 7 hours.
3. Stir this mix again, divide between plates and serve.

Enjoy!

Nutrition: calories 200, fat 3, fiber 7, carbs 13, protein 7

Beans, Carrots and Spinach Side Dish

Preparation time: 10 minutes
Cooking time: 4 hours
Servings: 6

Ingredients:

- 5 carrots, sliced
- 1 and ½ cups great northern beans, dried, soaked overnight and drained
- 2 garlic cloves, minced
- 1 yellow onion, chopped
- Salt and black pepper to the taste
- ½ teaspoon oregano, dried
- 5 ounces baby spinach
- 4 and ½ cups veggie stock
- 2 teaspoons lemon peel, grated
- 3 tablespoons lemon juice
- 1 avocado, pitted, peeled and chopped
- ¾ cup tofu, firm, pressed, drained and crumbled
- ¼ cup pistachios, chopped

Directions:

1. In your slow cooker, mix beans with onion, carrots, garlic, salt, pepper, oregano and veggie stock, stir, cover and cook on High for 4 hours.
2. Drain beans mix, return to your slow cooker and reserve ¼ cup cooking liquid.
3. Add spinach, lemon juice and lemon peel, stir and leave aside for 5 minutes.
4. Transfer beans, carrots and spinach mixture to a bowl, add pistachios, avocado, tofu and reserve cooking liquid, toss, divide between plates and serve as a side dish.

Enjoy!

Nutrition: calories 319, fat 8, fiber 14, carbs 43, protein 17

Scalloped Potatoes

Preparation time: 10 minutes
Cooking time: 4 hours
Servings: 8

Ingredients:

- Cooking spray
- 2 pounds gold potatoes, halved and sliced
- 1 yellow onion, cut into medium wedges
- 10 ounces canned vegan potato cream soup
- 8 ounces coconut milk
- 1 cup tofu, crumbled
- ½ cup veggie stock
- Salt and black pepper to the taste
- 1 tablespoons parsley, chopped

Directions:

1. Coat your slow cooker with cooking spray and arrange half of the potatoes on the bottom.
2. Layer onion wedges, half of the vegan cream soup, coconut milk, tofu, stock, salt and pepper.
3. Add the rest of the potatoes, onion wedges, cream, coconut milk, tofu and stock, cover and cook on High for 4 hours.
4. Sprinkle parsley on top, divide scalloped potatoes between plates and serve as a side dish.

Enjoy!

Nutrition: calories 306, fat 14, fiber 4, carbs 30, protein 12

Sweet Potatoes Side Dish

Preparation time: 10 minutes
Cooking time: 3 hours
Servings: 10

Ingredients:
- 4 pounds sweet potatoes, thinly sliced
- 3 tablespoons stevia
- ½ cup orange juice
- A pinch of salt and black pepper
- ½ teaspoon thyme, dried
- ½ teaspoon sage, dried
- 2 tablespoons olive oil

Directions:
1. Arrange potato slices on the bottom of your slow cooker.
2. In a bowl, mix orange juice with salt, pepper, stevia, thyme, sage and oil and whisk well.
3. Add this over potatoes, cover slow cooker and cook on High for 3 hours.
4. Divide between plates and serve as a side dish.
Enjoy!

Nutrition: calories 189, fat 4, fiber 4, carbs 36, protein 4

Cauliflower And Broccoli Side Dish

Preparation time: 10 minutes
Cooking time: 3 hours
Servings: 10

Ingredients:
- 4 cups broccoli florets
- 4 cups cauliflower florets
- 14 ounces tomato paste
- 1 yellow onion, chopped
- 1 teaspoon thyme, dried
- Salt and black pepper to the taste
- ½ cup almonds, sliced

Directions:
1. In your slow cooker, mix broccoli with cauliflower, tomato paste, onion, thyme, salt and pepper, toss, cover and cook on High for 3 hours.
2. Add almonds, toss, divide between plates and serve as a side dish.
Enjoy!

Nutrition: calories 177, fat 12, fiber 2, carbs 10, protein 7

Wild Rice Mix

Preparation time: 10 minutes
Cooking time: 6 hours
Servings: 12

Ingredients:
- 40 ounces veggie stock
- 2 and ½ cups wild rice
- 1 cup carrot, shredded
- 4 ounces mushrooms, sliced
- 2 tablespoons olive oil
- 2 teaspoons marjoram, dried and crushed
- Salt and black pepper to the taste
- 2/3 cup dried cherries
- ½ cup pecans, toasted and chopped
- 2/3 cup green onions, chopped

Directions:
1. In your slow cooker, mix stock with wild rice, carrot, mushrooms, oil, marjoram, salt, pepper, cherries, pecans and green onions, toss, cover and cook on Low for 6 hours.
2. Stir wild rice one more time, divide between plates and serve as a side dish.
Enjoy!

Nutrition: calories 169, fat 5, fiber 3, carbs 28, protein 5

Rustic Mashed Potatoes

Preparation time: 10 minutes
Cooking time: 4 hours
Servings: 6

Ingredients:
- 6 garlic cloves, peeled
- 3 pounds gold potatoes, peeled and cubed
- 1 bay leaf
- 1 cup coconut milk
- 28 ounces veggie stock
- 3 tablespoons olive oil
- Salt and black pepper to the taste

Directions:
1. In your slow cooker, mix potatoes with stock, bay leaf, garlic, salt and pepper, cover and cook on High for 4 hours.
2. Drain potatoes and garlic, return them to your slow cooker and mash using a potato masher.
3. Add oil and coconut milk, whisk well, divide between plates and serve as a side dish.
Enjoy!

Nutrition: calories 135, fat 5, fiber 1, carbs 20, protein 3

Glazed Carrots

Preparation time: 10 minutes
Cooking time: 4 hours
Servings: 10

Ingredients:
- 1 pound parsnips, cut into medium chunks
- 2 pounds carrots, cut into medium chunks
- 2 tablespoons orange peel, shredded
- 1 cup orange juice
- ½ cup orange marmalade
- ½ cup veggie stock
- 1 tablespoon tapioca, crushed
- A pinch of salt and black pepper
- 3 tablespoons olive oil
- ¼ cup parsley, chopped

Directions:
1. In your slow cooker, mix parsnips with carrots.
2. In a bowl, mix orange peel with orange juice, stock, orange marmalade, tapioca, salt and pepper, whisk and add over carrots.
3. Cover slow cooker and cook everything on High for 4 hours.
4. Add parsley, toss, divide between plates and serve as a side dish.

Enjoy!

Nutrition: calories 159, fat 4, fiber 4, carbs 30, protein 2

Mushroom And Peas Risotto

Preparation time: 10 minutes
Cooking time: 1 hour and 30 minutes
Servings: 8

Ingredients:
- 1 shallot, chopped
- 8 ounces white mushrooms, sliced
- 3 tablespoons olive oil
- 1 teaspoon garlic, minced
- 1 and ¾ cup white rice
- 4 cups veggie stock
- 1 cup peas
- Salt and black pepper to the taste

Directions:
1. In your slow cooker, mix oil with shallot, mushrooms, garlic, rice, stock, peas, salt and pepper, stir, cover and cook on High for 1 hour and 30 minutes.
2. Stir risotto one more time, divide between plates and serve as a side dish.

Enjoy!

Nutrition: calories 254, fat 7, fiber 3, carbs 27, protein 7

Squash And Spinach Mix

Preparation time: 10 minutes
Cooking time: 3 hours and 30 minutes
Servings: 12

Ingredients:

- 10 ounces spinach, torn
- 2 pounds butternut squash, peeled and cubed
- 1 cup barley
- 1 yellow onion, chopped
- 14 ounces veggie stock
- ½ cup water
- A pinch of salt and black pepper to the taste
- 3 garlic cloves, minced

Directions:

1. In your slow cooker, mix squash with spinach, barley, onion, stock, water, salt, pepper and garlic, toss, cover and cook on High for 3 hours and 30 minutes.
2. Divide squash mix on plates and serve as a side dish.

Enjoy!

Nutrition: calories 196, fat 3, fiber 7, carbs 36, protein 7

Chickpeas And Veggies

Preparation time: 10 minutes
Cooking time: 8 hours
Servings: 6

Ingredients:

- 30 ounces canned chickpeas, drained
- 2 tablespoons olive oil
- 2 tablespoons rosemary, chopped
- A pinch of salt and black pepper
- 2 cups cherry tomatoes, halved
- 2 garlic cloves, minced
- 1 cup corn
- 1 pound baby potatoes, peeled and halved
- 12 small baby carrots, peeled
- 28 ounces veggie stock
- 1 yellow onion, cut into medium wedges
- 4 cups baby spinach
- 8 ounces zucchini, sliced

Directions:

1. In your slow cooker, mix chickpeas with oil, rosemary, salt, pepper, cherry tomatoes, garlic, corn, baby potatoes, baby carrots, onion, zucchini, spinach and stock, stir, cover and cook on Low for 8 hours.
2. Divide everything between plates and serve as a side dish.

Enjoy!

Nutrition: calories 273, fat 7, fiber 11, carbs 38, protein 12

Eggplant And Kale Mix

Preparation time: 10 minutes
Cooking time: 2 hours
Servings: 6

Ingredients:

- 14 ounces canned roasted tomatoes and garlic
- 4 cups eggplant, cubed
- 1 yellow bell pepper, chopped
- 1 red onion, cut into medium wedges
- 4 cups kale leaves
- 2 tablespoons olive oil
- 1 teaspoon mustard
- 3 tablespoons red vinegar
- 1 garlic clove, minced
- A pinch of salt and black pepper
- ½ cup basil, chopped

Directions:

1. In your slow cooker, mix eggplant cubes with canned tomatoes, bell pepper and onion, toss, cover and cook on High for 2 hours.
2. Add kale, toss, cover slow cooker and leave aside for now.
3. Meanwhile, in a bowl, mix oil with vinegar, mustard, garlic, salt and pepper and whisk well.
4. Add this over eggplant mix, also add basil, toss, divide between plates and serve as a side dish.

Enjoy!

Nutrition: calories 251, fat 9, fiber 6, carbs 34, protein 8

Thai Veggie Mix

Preparation time: 10 minutes
Cooking time: 3 hours
Servings: 8

Ingredients:

- 8 ounces yellow summer squash, peeled and roughly chopped
- 12 ounces zucchini, halved and sliced
- 2 cups button mushrooms, quartered
- 1 red sweet potatoes, chopped
- 2 leeks, sliced
- 2 tablespoons veggie stock
- 2 garlic cloves, minced
- 2 tablespoon Thai red curry paste
- 1 tablespoon ginger, grated
- 1/3 cup coconut milk
- ¼ cup basil, chopped

Directions:

1. In your slow cooker, mix zucchini with summer squash, mushrooms, red pepper, leeks, garlic, stock, curry paste, ginger, coconut milk and basil, toss, cover and cook on Low for 3 hours.
2. Stir your Thai mix one more time, divide between plates and serve as a side dish.

Enjoy!

Nutrition: calories 69, fat 2, fiber 2, carbs 8, protein 2

Simple Potatoes Side Dish

Preparation time: 10 minutes
Cooking time: 3 hours
Servings: 12

Ingredients:
- 2 tablespoons olive oil
- 3 pounds new potatoes, halved
- 7 garlic cloves, minced
- 1 tablespoon rosemary, chopped
- A pinch of salt and black pepper

Directions:
1. In your slow cooker, mix oil with potatoes, garlic, rosemary, salt and pepper, toss, cover and cook on High for 3 hours.
2. Divide between plates and serve as a side dish.

Enjoy!

Nutrition: calories 102, fat 2, fiber 2, carbs 18, protein 2

Brussels Sprouts

Preparation time: 10 minutes
Cooking time: 3 hours
Servings: 12

Ingredients:
- 1 cup red onion, chopped
- 2 pounds Brussels sprouts, trimmed and halved
- A pinch of salt and black pepper
- ¼ cup apple juice
- 3 tablespoons olive oil
- ¼ cup maple syrup
- 1 tablespoon thyme, chopped

Directions:
1. In your slow cooker, mix Brussels sprouts with onion, salt, pepper and apple juice, toss, cover and cook on Low for 3 hours.
2. In a bowl, mix maple syrup with oil and thyme, whisk really well and add over Brussels sprouts.
3. Toss well, divide between plates and serve as a side dish.

Enjoy!

Nutrition: calories 100, fat 4, fiber 4, carbs 14, protein 3

Beets And Carrots

Preparation time: 10 minutes
Cooking time: 7 hours
Servings: 8

Ingredients:

- 2 tablespoons stevia
- ¾ cup pomegranate juice
- 2 teaspoons ginger, grated
- 2 and ½ pounds beets, peeled and cut into wedges
- 12 ounces carrots, cut into medium wedges

Directions:

1. In your slow cooker, mix beets with carrots, ginger, stevia and pomegranate juice, toss, cover and cook on Low for 7 hours.
2. Divide between plates and serve as a side dish.

Enjoy!

Nutrition: calories 125, fat 0, fiber 4, carbs 28, protein 3

Italian Veggie Side Dish

Preparation time: 10 minutes
Cooking time: 6 hours
Servings: 8

Ingredients:

- 38 ounces canned cannellini beans, drained
- 1 yellow onion, chopped
- ¼ cup basil pesto
- 19 ounces canned fava beans, drained
- 4 garlic cloves, minced
- 1 and ½ teaspoon Italian seasoning, dried and crushed
- 1 tomato, chopped
- 15 ounces already cooked polenta, cut into medium pieces
- 2 cups spinach
- 1 cup radicchio, torn

Directions:

1. In your slow cooker, mix cannellini beans with fava beans, basil pesto, onion, garlic, Italian seasoning, polenta, tomato, spinach and radicchio, toss, cover and cook on Low for 6 hours.
2. Divide between plates and serve as a side dish.

Enjoy!

Nutrition: calories 364, fat 12, fiber 10, carbs 45, protein 21

Acorn Squash And Great Sauce

Preparation time: 10 minutes
Cooking time: 6 hours
Servings: 4

Ingredients:

- 2 acorn squash, halved, deseeded and cut into medium wedges
- ¼ cup raisins
- 16 ounces cranberry sauce
- ¼ cup orange marmalade
- A pinch of salt and black pepper
- ¼ teaspoon cinnamon powder

Directions:

1. In your slow cooker, mix squash with raisins, cranberry sauce, orange marmalade, salt, pepper and cinnamon powder, toss, cover and cook on Low for 6 hours.
2. Stir again, divide between plates and serve as a side dish.

Enjoy!

Nutrition: calories 325, fat 6, fiber 3, carbs 28, protein 3

Pilaf

Preparation time: 10 minutes
Cooking time: 7 hours
Servings: 12

Ingredients:

- ½ cup wild rice
- ½ cup barley
- 2/3 cup wheat berries
- 27 ounces veggie stock
- 2 cups baby lima beans
- 1 red bell pepper, chopped
- 1 yellow onion, chopped
- 1 tablespoon olive oil
- A pinch of salt and black pepper
- 1 teaspoon sage, dried and crushed
- 4 garlic cloves, minced

Directions:

1. In your slow cooker, mix rice with barley, wheat berries, lima beans, bell pepper, onion, oil, salt, pepper, sage and garlic, stir, cover and cook on Low for 7 hours.
2. Stir one more time, divide between plates and serve as a side dish.

Enjoy!

Nutrition: calories 168, fat 5, fiber 4, carbs 25, protein 6

Special Potatoes Mix

Preparation time: 10 minutes
Cooking time: 7 hours
Servings: 10

Ingredients:
- 2 green apples, cored and cut into wedges
- 3 pounds sweet potatoes, peeled and cut into medium wedges
- 1 cup coconut cream
- ½ cup dried cherries
- 1 cup apple butter
- 1 and ½ teaspoon pumpkin pie spice

Directions:
1. In your slow cooker, mix sweet potatoes with green apples, cream, cherries, apple butter and spice, toss, cover and cook on Low for 7 hours.
2. Toss, divide between plates and serve as a side dish.

Enjoy!

Nutrition: calories 351, fat 8, fiber 5, carbs 48, protein 2

Creamy Corn

Preparation time: 10 minutes
Cooking time: 3 hours
Servings: 6

Ingredients:
- 50 ounces corn
- 1 cup almond milk
- 1 tablespoon stevia
- 8 ounces coconut cream
- A pinch of white pepper

Directions:
1. In your slow cooker, mix corn with almond milk, stevia, cream and white pepper, toss, cover and cook on High for 3 hours.
2. Divide between plates and serve as a side dish.

Enjoy!

Nutrition: calories 200, fat 5, fiber 7, carbs 12, protein 4

Vegan Slow Cooker Snack and Appetizer Recipes

Chipotle Tacos

Preparation time: 10 minutes
Cooking time: 4 hours
Servings: 4

Ingredients:

- 30 ounces canned pinto beans, drained
- ¾ cup chili sauce
- 3 ounces chipotle pepper in adobo sauce, chopped
- 1 cup corn
- 6 ounces tomato paste
- 1 tablespoon cocoa powder
- ½ teaspoon cinnamon, ground
- 1 teaspoon cumin, ground
- 8 vegan taco shells
- Chopped avocado, for serving

Directions:

1. Put the beans in your slow cooker.
2. Add chili sauce, chipotle pepper, corn, tomato paste, cocoa powder, cinnamon and cumin.
3. Stir, cover and cook on Low for 4 hours. Divide beans, chopped avocado into taco shells, and serve them.

Enjoy!

Nutrition: calories 342, fat 3, fiber 6, carbs 12, protein 10

Tasty Spinach Dip

Preparation time: 10 minutes
Cooking time: 4 hours
Servings: 12

Ingredients:

- 8 ounces baby spinach
- 1 small yellow onion, chopped
- 8 ounces vegan cashew mozzarella, shredded
- 8 ounces tofu, cubed
- 1 cup vegan cashew parmesan cheese, grated
- 1 tablespoon garlic, minced
- A pinch of cayenne pepper
- A pinch of sea salt
- Black pepper to the taste

Directions:

1. Put spinach in your slow cooker.
   Add onion, cashew mozzarella, tofu, cashew parmesan, salt, pepper, cayenne and garlic.
2. Stir, cover and cook on Low for 2 hours.
3. Stir your dip well, cover and cook on Low for 2 more hours.
4. Divide your spinach dip into bowls and serve.

Enjoy!

Nutrition: calories 200, fat 3, fiber 4, carbs 6, protein 8

Candied Almonds

Preparation time: 10 minutes
Cooking time: 4 hours
Servings: 10

Ingredients:

- 3 tablespoons cinnamon powder
- 3 cups palm sugar
- 4 and ½ cups almonds, raw
- ¼ cup water
- 2 teaspoons vanilla extract

Directions:

1. In a bowl, mix water with vanilla extract and whisk.
2. In another bowl, mix cinnamon with sugar and stir.
3. Dip almonds in water, then add them to the bowl with the cinnamon sugar.
4. Toss to coat really well, add almonds to your slow cooker, cover and cook on Low for 4 hours, stirring often.
5. Divide into bowls and serve as a snack.

Enjoy!

Nutrition: calories 150, fat 3, fiber 4, carbs 6, protein 8

Eggplant Tapenade

Preparation time: 10 minutes
Cooking time: 7 hours
Servings: 6

Ingredients:

- 1 and ½ cups tomatoes, chopped
- 3 cups eggplant, chopped
- 2 teaspoons capers
- 4 garlic cloves, minced
- 1 tablespoon basil, chopped
- 2 teaspoons balsamic vinegar
- A pinch of sea salt
- Black pepper to the taste
- 6 ounces green olives, pitted and sliced

Directions:

1. Put tomatoes and eggplant pieces in your slow cooker.
2. Add garlic, capers, basil and olives, stir, cover and cook on Low for 7 hours.
3. Add salt, pepper, vinegar, stir gently, divide into small bowls and serve as an appetizer.

Enjoy!

Nutrition: calories 140, fat 3, fiber 5, carbs 7, protein 5

Almond and Beans Fondue

Preparation time: 10 minutes
Cooking time: 8 hours
Servings: 4

Ingredients:

- ½ cup almonds
- 1 and ¼ cups water
- 1 teaspoon nutritional yeast flakes
- ¼ cup great northern beans
- A pinch of sea salt
- Black pepper to the taste
- Baby carrots, steamed for serving
- Tofu cubes for serving

Directions:

1. Put the water in your slow cooker.
2. Add almonds and beans, stir, cover and cook on Low for 8 hours.
3. Transfer these to your blender, add yeast flakes, a pinch of salt and black pepper and pulse really well.
4. Transfer to bowls and serve with baby carrots and tofu cubes on the side.

Enjoy!

Nutrition: calories 200, fat 4, fiber 4, carbs 8, protein 10

Beans in Rich Tomato Sauce

Preparation time: 10 minutes
Cooking time: 8 hours and 10 minutes
Servings: 6

Ingredients:

- 1 pound lima beans, soaked for 6 hours and drained
- 2 celery ribs, chopped
- 2 tablespoons olive oil
- 2 onions, chopped
- 2 carrots, chopped
- 4 tablespoons tomato paste
- 3 garlic cloves, minced
- A pinch of sea salt
- Black pepper to the taste
- 7 cups water
- 1 bay leaf
- 1 teaspoon oregano, dried
- ½ teaspoon thyme, dried
- A pinch of red pepper, crushed
- ¼ cup parsley, chopped
- 1 cup cashew cheese, shredded

Directions:

1. Heat up a pan with the oil over medium high heat, add onions, stir and cook for 4 minutes.
2. Add garlic, celery, carrots, salt and pepper, stir, cook for 4-5 minutes more and transfer to your slow cooker.
3. Add beans, tomato paste, water, bay leaf, oregano, thyme and red pepper, stir, cover and cook on Low for 8 hours.
4. Add parsley, stir, divide into bowls and serve cold with cashew cheese on top.

Enjoy!

Nutrition: calories 160, fat 3, fiber 7, carbs 9, protein 12

Tasty Onion Dip

Preparation time: 10 minutes
Cooking time: 8 hours
Servings: 6

Ingredients:

- 3 cups yellow onions, chopped
- A pinch of sea salt
- 2 tablespoons olive oil
- 1 tablespoon coconut butter
- 1 cup coconut milk
- ½ cup avocado mayonnaise
- A pinch of cayenne pepper

Directions:

1. Put the onions in your slow cooker.
2. Add a pinch of salt, oil and coconut butter, stir well, cover and cook on High for 8 hours.
3. Drain excess liquid, transfer onion to a bowl, add coconut milk, avocado mayo and cayenne, stir really well and serve with potato chips on the side.

Enjoy!

Nutrition: calories 200, fat 4, fiber 4, carbs 9, protein 7

Special Beans Dip

Preparation time: 10 minutes
Cooking time: 2 hours
Servings: 20

Ingredients:

- 16 ounces canned beans, drained
- 1 cup mild hot sauce
- 2 cups cashew cheese, shredded
- ¾ cup coconut milk
- ¼ teaspoon cumin, ground
- 1 tablespoon chili powder
- 3 ounces tofu, cubed

Directions:

1. Put beans in your slow cooker.
2. Add hot sauce, cashew cheese, coconut milk, cumin, tofu and chili powder.
3. Stir, cover and cook for 2 hours.
4. Stir halfway.
5. Transfer to bowls and serve with corn chips on the side.

Enjoy!

Nutrition: calories 230, fat 4, fiber 6, carbs 8, protein 10

Sweet and Spicy Nuts

Preparation time: 10 minutes
Cooking time: 2 hours
Servings: 20

Ingredients:

- 1 cup almonds, toasted
- 1 cup cashews
- 1 cup pecans, halved and toasted
- 1 cup hazelnuts, toasted and peeled
- ½ cup palm sugar
- 1 teaspoon ginger, grated
- 1/3 cup coconut butter, melted
- ½ teaspoon cinnamon powder
- ¼ teaspoon cloves, ground
- A pinch of salt
- A pinch of cayenne pepper

Directions:

1. Put almonds, pecans, cashews and hazelnuts in your slow cooker.
2. Add palm sugar, coconut butter, ginger, salt, cayenne, cloves and cinnamon.
3. Stir well, cover and cook on Low for 2 hours.
4. Divide into bowls and serve as a snack.

Enjoy!

Nutrition: calories 110, fat 3, fiber 2, carbs 5, protein 5

Delicious Corn Dip

Preparation time: 10 minutes
Cooking time: 2 hours and 15 minutes
Servings: 8

Ingredients:

- 2 jalapenos, chopped
- 45 ounces canned corn kernels, drained
- ½ cup coconut milk
- 1 and ¼ cups cashew cheese, shredded
- A pinch of sea salt
- Black pepper to the taste
- 2 tablespoons chives, chopped
- 8 ounces tofu, cubed

Directions:

1. In your slow cooker, mix coconut milk with cashew cheese, corn, jalapenos, tofu, salt and pepper, stir, cover and cook on Low for 2 hours.
2. Stir your corn dip really well, cover slow cooker again and cook on High for 15 minutes.
3. Divide into bowls, sprinkle chives on top and serve as a vegan snack!

Enjoy!

Nutrition: calories 150, fat 3, fiber 2, carbs 8, protein 10

Butternut Squash Spread

Preparation time: 10 minutes
Cooking time: 6 hours
Servings: 4

Ingredients:
- ½ cup butternut squash, peeled and cubed
- ½ cup canned white beans, drained
- 1 tablespoon water
- 2 tablespoons coconut milk
- A pinch of rosemary, dried
- A pinch of sage, dried
- A pinch of salt and black pepper

Directions:
1. In your slow cooker, mix beans with squash, water, coconut milk, sage, rosemary, salt and pepper, toss, cover and cook on Low for 6 hours.
2. Blend using an immersion blender, divide into bowls and serve cold as a party spread.

Enjoy!

Nutrition: calories 182, fat 5, fiber 7, carbs 12, protein 5

Cashew And White Bean Spread

Preparation time: 10 minutes
Cooking time: 7 hours
Servings: 4

Ingredients:
- ½ cup white beans, dried
- 2 tablespoons cashews, soaked for 12 hours and blended
- 1 teaspoon apple cider vinegar
- 1 cup veggie stock
- 1 tablespoon water

Directions:
1. In your slow cooker, mix beans with cashews and stock, stir, cover and cook on Low for 6 hours.
2. Drain, transfer to your food processor, add vinegar and water, pulse well, divide into bowls and serve as a spread.

Enjoy!

Nutrition: calories 221, fat 6, fiber 5, carbs 19, protein 3

Vegan Rolls

Preparation time: 10 minutes
Cooking time: 8 hours
Servings: 4

Ingredients:
- 1 cup brown lentils, cooked
- 1 green cabbage head, leaves separated
- ½ cup onion, chopped
- 1 cup brown rice, already cooked
- 2 ounces white mushrooms, chopped
- ¼ cup pine nuts, toasted
- ¼ cup raisins
- 2 garlic cloves, minced
- 2 tablespoons dill, chopped
- 1 tablespoon olive oil
- 25 ounces marinara sauce
- A pinch of salt and black pepper
- ¼ cup water

Directions:
1. In a bowl, mix lentils with onion, rice, mushrooms, pine nuts, raisins, garlic, dill, salt and pepper and whisk well.
2. Arrange cabbage leaves on a working surface, divide lentils mix and wrap them well.
3. Add marinara sauce and water to your slow cooker and stir.
4. Add cabbage rolls, cover and cook on Low for 8 hours.
5. Arrange cabbage rolls on a platter, drizzle sauce all over and serve.

Enjoy!

Nutrition: calories 261, fat 6, fiber 6, carbs 12, protein 3

Eggplant Appetizer

Preparation time: 10 minutes
Cooking time: 7 hours
Servings: 4

Ingredients:
- 1 and ½ cups tomatoes, chopped
- 3 cups eggplant, cubed
- 2 teaspoons capers
- 6 ounces green olives, pitted and sliced
- 4 garlic cloves, minced
- 2 teaspoons balsamic vinegar
- 1 tablespoon basil, chopped
- Salt and black pepper to the taste

Directions:
1. In your slow cooker, mix tomatoes with eggplant cubes, capers, green olives, garlic, vinegar, basil, salt and pepper, toss, cover and cook on Low for 7 hours.
2. Divide into small appetizer plates and serve as an appetizer.

Enjoy!

Nutrition: calories 200, fat 6, fiber 5, carbs 9, protein 2

Vegan Veggie Dip

Preparation time: 10 minutes
Cooking time: 7 hours
Servings: 4

Ingredients:

- 1 cup carrots, sliced
- 1 and ½ cups cauliflower florets
- 1/3 cup cashews
- ½ cup turnips, chopped
- 2 and ½ cups water
- 1 cup almond milk
- 1 teaspoon garlic powder
- ¼ cup nutritional yeast
- ¼ teaspoon smoked paprika
- ¼ teaspoon mustard powder
- A pinch of salt

Directions:

1. In your slow cooker, mix carrots with cauliflower, cashews, turnips and water, stir, cover and cook on Low for 7 hours.
2. Drain, transfer to a blender, add almond milk, garlic powder, yeast, paprika, mustard powder and salt, blend well and serve as a snack.

Enjoy!

Nutrition: calories 291, fat 7, fiber 4, carbs 14, protein 3

Great Bolognese Dip

Preparation time: 10 minutes
Cooking time: 5 hours
Servings: 7

Ingredients:

- ½ cauliflower head, riced in your blender
- 54 ounces canned tomatoes, crushed
- 10 ounces white mushrooms, chopped
- 2 cups carrots, shredded
- 2 cups eggplant, cubed
- 6 garlic cloves, minced
- 2 tablespoons agave nectar
- 2 tablespoons balsamic vinegar
- 2 tablespoons tomato paste
- 1 tablespoon basil, chopped
- 1 and ½ tablespoons oregano, chopped
- 1 and ½ teaspoons rosemary, dried
- A pinch of salt and black pepper

Directions:

1. In your slow cooker, mix cauliflower rice with tomatoes, mushrooms, carrots, eggplant cubes, garlic, agave nectar, balsamic vinegar, tomato paste, rosemary, salt and pepper, stir, cover and cook on High for 5 hours.
2. Add basil and oregano, stir again, divide into bowls and serve as a dip.

Enjoy!

Nutrition: calories 251, fat 7, fiber 6, carbs 10, protein 6

Black Eyed Peas Pate

Preparation time: 10 minutes
Cooking time: 5 hours
Servings: 5

Ingredients:

- 1 and ½ cups black-eyed peas
- 3 cups water
- 1 teaspoon Cajun seasoning
- ½ cup pecans, toasted
- ½ teaspoon garlic powder
- ½ teaspoon jalapeno powder
- A pinch of salt and black pepper
- ¼ teaspoon liquid smoke
- ½ teaspoon Tabasco sauce

Directions:

1. In your slow cooker, mix black-eyed pea with Cajun seasoning, salt, pepper and water, stir, cover and cook on High for 5 hours.
2. Drain, transfer to a blender, add pecans, garlic powder, jalapeno powder, Tabasco sauce, liquid smoke, more salt and pepper, pulse well and serve as an appetizer.

Enjoy!

Nutrition: calories 221, fat 4, fiber 7, carbs 16, protein 4

Tofu Appetizer

Preparation time: 10 minutes
Cooking time: 7 hours
Servings: 6

Ingredients:

- ¼ cup yellow onions, sliced
- 1 cup carrot, sliced
- 14 ounces firm tofu, cubed

For the sauce:

- ¼ cup soy sauce
- ½ cup water
- 3 tablespoons agave nectar
- 3 tablespoons nutritional yeast
- 1 teaspoon garlic, minced
- 1 tablespoon ginger, minced
- ½ tablespoon rice vinegar

Directions:

1. In your slow cooker, mix tofu with onion and carrots.
2. In a bowl, mix soy sauce with water, agave nectar, yeast, garlic, ginger and vinegar and whisk well.
3. Add this to slow cooker, cover and cook on Low for 7 hours.
4. Divide into appetizer bowls and serve.

Enjoy!

Nutrition: calories 251, fat 6, fiber 8, carbs 12, protein 3

Hummus

Preparation time: 10 minutes
Cooking time: 8 hours
Servings: 10

Ingredients:

- 1 cup chickpeas, dried
- 2 tablespoons olive oil
- 3 cups water
- A pinch of salt and black pepper
- 1 garlic clove, minced
- 1 tablespoon lemon juice

Directions:

1. In your slow cooker, mix chickpeas with water, salt and pepper, stir, cover and cook on Low for 8 hours.
2. Drain chickpeas, transfer to a blender, add oil, more salt and pepper, garlic and lemon juice, blend well, divide into bowls and serve.

Enjoy!

Nutrition: calories 211, fat 6, fiber 7, carbs 8, protein 4

Vegan Cashew Spread

Preparation time: 10 minutes
Cooking time: 3 hours
Servings: 10

Ingredients:

- 1 cup water
- 1 cup cashews
- 10 ounces vegan hummus
- ¼ teaspoon garlic powder
- ¼ teaspoon onion powder
- ¼ cup nutritional yeast
- A pinch of salt and black pepper
- ¼ teaspoon mustard powder
- 1 teaspoon apple cider vinegar

Directions:

1. In your slow cooker, mix water with cashews, yeast, salt and pepper, stir, cover and cook on High for 3 hours.
2. Transfer to your blender, add hummus, garlic powder, onion powder, mustard powder and vinegar, pulse well, divide into bowls and serve.

Enjoy!

Nutrition: calories 192, fat 7, fiber 7, carbs 12, protein 4

Spinach Dip

Preparation time: 10 minutes
Cooking time: 30 minutes
Servings: 4

Ingredients:
- ½ cup coconut cream
- ¾ cup coconut yogurt
- 10 ounces spinach leaves
- 8 ounces water chestnuts, chopped
- 1 garlic clove, minced
- Black pepper to the taste

Directions:
1. In your slow cooker, mix coconut cream with spinach, coconut yogurt, chestnuts, black pepper and garlic, stir, cover and cook on High for 30 minutes.
2. Blend using an immersion blender, divide into bowls and serve.

Enjoy!

Nutrition: calories 221, fat 5, fiber 7, carbs 12, protein 5

Chowder

Preparation time: 10 minutes
Cooking time: 8 hours
Servings: 8

Ingredients:
- 2 cups corn
- 2 cups potatoes, peeled and cubed
- 4 cups veggie stock
- 2 carrots, chopped
- 2 celery stalks, chopped
- 1 yellow onion, chopped
- A pinch of salt and black pepper
- 1 cup coconut cream
- 1 teaspoon thyme, dried
- 4 zucchinis, chopped
- ½ cup basil, chopped
- 3 tomatoes, chopped

Directions:
1. In your slow cooker, mix stock with corn, potatoes, carrot, celery, onion, salt, pepper, cream, zucchini and thyme, stir, cover and cook on Low for 8 hours.
2. Blend using an immersion blender, add basil and tomatoes, stir, divide into small bowls and serve as an appetizer.

Enjoy!

Nutrition: calories 311, fat 6, fiber 7, carbs 12, protein 4

Appetizer Potato Salad

Preparation time: 10 minutes
Cooking time: 8 hours
Servings: 6

Ingredients:
- 1 sweet onion, chopped
- ¼ cup white vinegar
- 2 tablespoons mustard
- A pinch of salt and black pepper
- 1 and ½ pounds gold potatoes, cut into medium chunks
- ¼ cup dill, chopped
- 1 cup celery, chopped
- Cooking spray

Directions:
1. Spray your slow cooker with cooking spray, add onion, vinegar, mustard, salt and pepper and whisk well.
2. Add celery and potatoes, toss them well, cover and cook on Low for 8 hours.
3. Divide salad into small bowls, sprinkle dill on top and serve as an appetizer.

Enjoy!

Nutrition: calories 251, fat 6, fiber 7, carbs 8, protein 7

Veggie Appetizer

Preparation time: 10 minutes
Cooking time: 3 hours
Servings: 4

Ingredients:
- 2 red bell peppers, cut into medium wedges
- 1 sweet potato, cut into medium wedges
- 3 zucchinis, sliced
- ½ cup garlic, minced
- 2 tablespoons olive oil
- A pinch of salt and black pepper
- 1 teaspoon Italian seasoning

Directions:
1. In your slow cooker, mix bell peppers with sweet potato, zucchinis, garlic, oil, salt, pepper and seasoning, toss, cover and cook on High for 3 hours.
2. Divide into small bowls and serve cold as an appetizer.

Enjoy!

Nutrition: calories 132, fat 3, fiber 3, carbs 4, protein 4

Black Bean Appetizer Salad

Preparation time: 10 minutes
Cooking time: 4 hours
Servings: 7

Ingredients:
- 1 tablespoon coconut aminos
- ½ teaspoon cumin, ground
- 1 cup canned black beans
- 1 cup salsa
- 6 cups romaine lettuce leaves
- ½ cup avocado, peeled, pitted and mashed

Directions:
1. In your slow cooker, mix black beans with salsa, cumin and aminos, stir, cover and cook on Low for 4 hours.
2. In a salad bowl, mix lettuce leaves with black beans mix and mashed avocado, toss and serve as an appetizer.

Enjoy!

Nutrition: calories 221, fat 4, fiber 7, carbs 12, protein 3

Coloured Stuffed Bell Peppers

Preparation time: 10 minutes
Cooking time: 4 hours
Servings: 5

Ingredients:
- 1 yellow onion, chopped
- 2 teaspoons olive oil
- 2 celery ribs, chopped
- 1 tablespoon chili powder
- 3 garlic cloves, minced
- 2 teaspoon cumin, ground
- 1 and ½ teaspoon oregano, dried
- 2 cups white rice, already cooked
- 1 cup corn
- 1 tomato chopped
- 7 ounces canned pinto beans, drained
- 1 chipotle pepper in adobo
- A pinch of salt and black pepper
- 5 colored bell peppers, tops and insides scooped out
- ½ cup vegan enchilada sauce

Directions:
1. Heat up a pan with the oil over medium high heat, add onion and celery, stir and cook for 5 minutes.
2. Add garlic, stir, cook for 1 minute more, take off heat and mix with chili, cumin and oregano.
3. Also add rice, corn, beans, tomato, salt, pepper and chipotle pepper and stir well.
4. Stuff bell peppers with this mix and place them in your slow cooker.
5. Add enchilada sauce, cover and cook on Low for 4 hours.
6. Arrange stuffed bell peppers on a platter and serve them as an appetizer.

Enjoy!

Nutrition: calories 221, fat 5, fiber 4, carbs 19, protein 3

Corn Dip

Preparation time: 10 minutes
Cooking time: 2 hours
Servings: 8

Ingredients:
- 30 ounces canned corn, drained
- 2 green onions, chopped
- ½ cup coconut cream
- 8 ounces tofu, crumbled
- 1 jalapeno, chopped
- ½ teaspoon chili powder

Directions:
1. In your slow cooker, mix corn with green onions, coconut cream, tofu, chili powder and jalapeno, stir, cover and cook on Low for 2 hours.
2. Divide into bowls and serve as a dip.

Enjoy!

Nutrition: calories 332, fat 5, fiber 10, carbs 17, protein 4

Artichoke Spread

Preparation time: 10 minutes
Cooking time: 2 hours
Servings: 8

Ingredients:
- 28 ounces canned artichokes, drained and chopped
- 10 ounces spinach
- 8 ounces coconut cream
- 1 yellow onion, chopped
- 2 garlic cloves, minced
- ¾ cup coconut milk
- ½ cup tofu, pressed and crumbled
- 1/3 cup vegan avocado mayonnaise
- 1 tablespoon red vinegar
- A pinch of salt and black pepper

Directions:
1. In your slow cooker, mix artichokes with spinach, coconut cream, onion, garlic, coconut milk, tofu, avocado mayo, vinegar, salt and pepper, stir well, cover and cook on Low for 2 hours.
2. Divide into bowls and serve as an appetizer.

Enjoy!

Nutrition: calories 355, fat 24, fiber 4, carbs 19, protein 13

Mushroom Spread

Preparation time: 10 minutes
Cooking time: 4 hours
Servings: 6

Ingredients:

- 2 cups green bell peppers, chopped
- 1 cup yellow onion, chopped
- 3 garlic cloves, minced
- 1 pound mushrooms, chopped
- 28 ounces tomato sauce
- ½ cup tofu, pressed, drained and crumbled
- Salt and black pepper to the taste

Directions:

1. In your slow cooker, mix bell peppers with onion, garlic, mushrooms, tomato sauce, tofu, salt and pepper, stir, cover and cook on Low for 4 hours.
2. Divide into bowls and serve as a party spread.

Enjoy!

Nutrition: calories 245, fat 4, fiber 7, carbs 9, protein 3

Three Bean Dip

Preparation time: 10 minutes
Cooking time: 1 hour
Servings: 6

Ingredients:

- ½ cup salsa
- 2 cups canned refried beans
- 1 cup vegan nacho cheese
- 2 tablespoons green onions, chopped

Directions:

1. In your slow cooker, mix refried beans with salsa, vegan nacho cheese and green onions, stir, cover and cook on High for 1 hour.
2. Divide into bowls and serve as a party snack.

Enjoy!

Nutrition: calories 262, fat 5, fiber 10, carbs 20, protein 3

Vegan Slow Cooker Main Dish Recipes

Classic Black Beans Chili

Preparation time: 10 minutes
Cooking time: 3 hours
Servings: 4

Ingredients:

- ½ cup quinoa
- 2 and ½ cups veggie stock
- 14 ounces canned tomatoes, chopped
- 15 ounces canned black beans, drained
- ¼ cup green bell pepper, chopped
- ¼ cup red bell pepper, chopped
- A pinch of salt and black pepper
- 2 garlic cloves, minced
- 1 carrots, shredded
- 1 small chili pepper, chopped
- 2 teaspoons chili powder
- 1 teaspoon cumin, ground
- A pinch of cayenne pepper
- ½ cup corn
- 1 teaspoon oregano, dried
  For the vegan sour cream:
- A drizzle of apple cider vinegar
- 4 tablespoons water
- ½ cup cashews, soaked overnight and drained
- 1 teaspoon lime juice

Directions:

1. Put the stock in your slow cooker.
2. Add quinoa, tomatoes, beans, red and green bell pepper, garlic, carrot, salt, pepper, corn, cumin, cayenne, chili powder, chili pepper and oregano, stir, cover and cook on High for 3 hours.
3. Meanwhile, put the cashews in your blender.
4. Add water, vinegar and lime juice and pulse really well.
5. Divide beans chili into bowls, top with vegan sour cream and serve.

Enjoy!

Nutrition: calories 300, fat 4, fiber 4, carbs 10, protein 7

Amazing Potato Dish

Preparation time: 10 minutes
Cooking time: 3 hours
Servings: 4

Ingredients:

- 1 and ½ pounds potatoes, peeled and roughly chopped
- 1 tablespoon olive oil
- 3 tablespoons water
- 1 small yellow onion, chopped
- ½ cup veggie stock cube, crumbled
- ½ teaspoon coriander, ground
- ½ teaspoon cumin, ground
- ½ teaspoon garam masala
- ½ teaspoon chili powder
- Black pepper to the taste
- ½ pound spinach, roughly torn

Directions:

1. Put the potatoes in your slow cooker.
2. Add oil, water, onion, stock cube, coriander, cumin, garam masala, chili powder, black pepper and spinach.
3. Stir, cover and cook on High for 3 hours.
4. Divide into bowls and serve.

Enjoy!

Nutrition: calories 270, fat 4, fiber 6, carbs 8, protein 12

Textured Sweet Potatoes and Lentils Delight

Preparation time: 10 minutes
Cooking time: 4 hours and 30 minutes
Servings: 6

Ingredients:

- 6 cups sweet potatoes, peeled and cubed
- 2 teaspoons coriander, ground
- 2 teaspoons chili powder
- 1 yellow onion, chopped
- 3 cups veggie stock
- 4 garlic cloves, minced
- A pinch of sea salt and black pepper
- 10 ounces canned coconut milk
- 1 cup water
- 1 and ½ cups red lentils

Directions:

1. Put sweet potatoes in your slow cooker.
2. Add coriander, chili powder, onion, stock, garlic, salt and pepper, stir, cover and cook on High for 3 hours.
3. Add lentils, stir, cover and cook for 1 hour and 30 minutes.
4. Add water and coconut milk, stir well, divide into bowls and serve right away.

Enjoy!

Nutrition: calories 300, fat 10, fiber 8, carbs 16, protein 10

Incredibly Tasty Pizza

Preparation time: 1 hour and 10 minutes
Cooking time: 1 hour and 45 minutes
Servings: 3
Ingredients:

For the dough:
- ½ teaspoon Italian seasoning
- 1 and ½ cups whole wheat flour
- 1 and ½ teaspoons instant yeast
- 1 tablespoon olive oil
- A pinch of salt
- ½ cup warm water
- Cooking spray

For the sauce:
- ¼ cup green olives, pitted and sliced
- ¼ cup kalamata olives, pitted and sliced
- ½ cup tomatoes, crushed
- 1 tablespoon parsley, chopped
- 1 tablespoon capers, rinsed
- ¼ teaspoon garlic powder
- ¼ teaspoon basil, dried
- ¼ teaspoon oregano, dried
- ¼ teaspoon palm sugar
- ¼ teaspoon red pepper flakes
- A pinch of salt and black pepper
- ½ cup cashew mozzarella, shredded

Directions:

1. In your food processor, mix yeast with Italian seasoning, a pinch of salt and flour.
2. Add oil and the water and blend well until you obtain a dough.
3. Transfer dough to a floured working surface, knead well, transfer to a greased bowl, cover and leave aside for 1 hour.
4. Meanwhile, in a bowl, mix green olives with kalamata olives, tomatoes, parsley, capers, garlic powder, oregano, sugar, salt, pepper and pepper flakes and stir well.
5. Transfer pizza dough to a working surface again and flatten it.
6. Shape so it will fit your slow cooker.
7. Grease your slow cooker with cooking spray and add dough.
8. Press well on the bottom.
9. Spread the sauce mix all over, cover and cook on High for 1 hour and 15 minutes.
10. Spread vegan mozzarella all over, cover again and cook on High for 30 minutes more.
11. Leave your pizza to cool down before slicing and serving it.

Nutrition: calories 340, fat 5, fiber 7, carbs 13, protein 15

Rich Beans Soup

Preparation time: 10 minutes
Cooking time: 7 hours
Servings: 4

Ingredients:

- 1 pound navy beans
- 1 yellow onion, chopped
- 4 garlic cloves, crushed
- 2 quarts veggie stock
- A pinch of sea salt
- Black pepper to the taste
- 2 potatoes, peeled and cubed
- 2 teaspoons dill, dried
- 1 cup sun-dried tomatoes, chopped
- 1 pound carrots, sliced
- 4 tablespoons parsley, minced

Directions:

1. Put the stock in your slow cooker.
2. Add beans, onion, garlic, potatoes, tomatoes, carrots, dill, salt and pepper, stir, cover and cook on Low for 7 hours.
3. Stir your soup, add parsley, divide into bowls and serve.

Nutrition: calories 250, fat 4, fiber 3, carbs 9, protein 10

Delicious Baked Beans

Preparation time: 10 minutes
Cooking time: 12 hours
Servings: 8

Ingredients:

- 1 pound navy beans, soaked overnight and drained
- 1 cup maple syrup
- 1 cup bourbon
- 1 cup vegan bbq sauce
- 1 cup palm sugar
- ¼ cup ketchup
- 1 cup water
- ¼ cup mustard
- ¼ cup blackstrap molasses
- ¼ cup apple cider vinegar
- ¼ cup olive oil
- 2 tablespoons coconut aminos

Directions:

1. Put the beans in your slow cooker.
2. Add maple syrup, bourbon, bbq sauce, sugar, ketchup, water, mustard, molasses, vinegar, oil and coconut aminos.
3. Stir everything, cover and cook on Low for 12 hours.
4. Divide into bowls and serve.

Enjoy!

Nutrition: calories 430, fat 7, fiber 8, carbs 15, protein 19

Indian Lentils

Preparation time: 10 minutes
Cooking time: 3 hours
Servings: 4

Ingredients:

- 1 yellow bell pepper, chopped
- 1 sweet potato, chopped
- 2 and ½ cups lentils, already cooked
- 4 garlic cloves, minced
- 1 yellow onion, chopped
- 2 teaspoons cumin, ground
- 15 ounces canned tomato sauce
- ½ teaspoon ginger, ground
- A pinch of cayenne pepper
- 1 tablespoons coriander, ground
- 1 teaspoon turmeric, ground
- 2 teaspoons paprika
- 2/3 cup veggie stock
- 1 teaspoon garam masala
- A pinch of sea salt
- Black pepper to the taste
- Juice of 1 lemon

Directions:

1. Put the stock in your slow cooker.
2. Add potato, lentils, onion, garlic, cumin, bell pepper, tomato sauce, salt, pepper, ginger, coriander, turmeric, paprika, cayenne, garam masala and lemon juice.
3. Stir, cover and cook on High for 3 hours.
4. Stir your lentils mix again, divide into bowls and serve.

Enjoy!

Nutrition: calories 300, fat 6, fiber 5, carbs 9, protein 12

Delicious Butternut Squash Soup

Preparation time: 10 minutes
Cooking time: 6 hours
Servings: 8

Ingredients:

- 1 apple, cored, peeled and chopped
- ½ pound carrots, chopped
- 1 pound butternut squash, peeled and cubed
- 1 yellow onion, chopped
- A pinch of sea salt
- Black pepper to the taste
- 1 bay leaf
- 3 cups veggie stock
- 14 ounces canned coconut milk
- ¼ teaspoon sage, dried

Directions:

1. Put the stock in your slow cooker.
2. Add apple squash, carrots, onion, salt, pepper and bay leaf.
3. Stir, cover and cook on Low for 6 hours.
4. Transfer to your blender, add coconut milk and sage and pulse really well.
5. Ladle into bowls and serve right away.

Enjoy!

Nutrition: calories 200, fat 3, fiber 6, carbs 8, protein 10

Amazing Mushroom Stew

Preparation time: 10 minutes
Cooking time: 8 hours
Servings: 4

Ingredients:

- 2 garlic cloves, minced
- 1 celery stalk, chopped
- 1 yellow onion, chopped
- 1 and ½ cups firm tofu, pressed and cubed
- 1 cup water
- 10 ounces mushrooms, chopped
- 1 pound mixed peas, corn and carrots
- 2 and ½ cups veggie stock
- 1 teaspoon thyme, dried
- 2 tablespoons coconut flour
- A pinch of sea salt
- Black pepper to the taste

Directions:

1. Put the water and stock in your slow cooker.
2. Add garlic, onion, celery, mushrooms, mixed veggies, tofu, thyme, salt, pepper and flour.
3. Stir everything, cover and cook on Low for 8 hours.
4. Divide into bowls and serve hot.

Enjoy!

Nutrition: calories 230, fat 4, fiber 6, carbs 10, protein 7

Simple Tofu Dish

Preparation time: 10 minutes
Cooking time: 3 hours
Servings: 6

Ingredients:

- 1 big tofu package, cubed
- 1 tablespoon sesame oil
- ¼ cup pineapple, cubed
- 1 tablespoon olive oil
- 2 garlic cloves, minced
- 1 tablespoons brown rice vinegar
- 2 teaspoon ginger, grated
- ¼ cup soy sauce
- 5 big zucchinis, cubed
- ¼ cup sesame seeds

Directions:

1. In your food processor, mix sesame oil with pineapple, olive oil, garlic, ginger, soy sauce and vinegar and whisk well.
2. Add this to your slow cooker and mix with tofu cubes.
3. Cover and cook on High for 2 hours and 45 minutes.
4. Add sesame seeds and zucchinis, stir gently, cover and cook on High for 15 minutes.
5. Divide between plates and serve.

Enjoy!

Nutrition: calories 200, fat 3, fiber 4, carbs 9, protein 10

Special Jambalaya

Preparation time: 10 minutes
Cooking time: 6 hours
Servings: 4

Ingredients:

- 6 ounces soy chorizo, chopped
- 1 and ½ cups celery ribs, chopped
- 1 cup okra
- 1 green bell pepper, chopped
- 16 ounces canned tomatoes and green chilies, chopped
- 2 garlic cloves, minced
- ½ teaspoon paprika
- 1 and ½ cups veggie stock
- A pinch of cayenne pepper
- Black pepper to the taste
- A pinch of salt
- 3 cups already cooked wild rice for serving

Directions:

1. Heat up a pan over medium high heat, add soy chorizo, stir, brown for a few minutes and transfer to your slow cooker.
2. Also, add celery, bell pepper, okra, tomatoes and chilies, garlic, paprika, salt, pepper and cayenne to your slow cooker.
3. Stir everything, add veggie stock, cover the slow cooker and cook on Low for 6 hours.
4. Divide rice on plates, top each serving with your vegan jambalaya and serve hot.

Enjoy!

Nutrition: calories 150, fat 3, fiber 7, carbs 15, protein 9

Delicious Chard Soup

Preparation time: 10 minutes
Cooking time: 8 hours
Servings: 6

Ingredients:

- 1 yellow onion, chopped
- 1 tablespoon olive oil
- 1 celery stalk, chopped
- 2 garlic cloves, minced
- 1 carrot, chopped
- 1 bunch Swiss chard, torn
- 1 cup brown lentils, dried
- 5 potatoes, peeled and cubed
- 1 tablespoon soy sauce
- Black pepper to the taste
- A pinch of sea salt
- 6 cups veggie stock

Directions:

1. Heat up a big pan with the oil over medium high heat, add onion, celery, garlic, carrot and Swiss chard, stir, cook for a few minutes and transfer to your slow cooker.
2. Also, add lentils, potatoes, soy sauce, salt, pepper and stock to the slow cooker, stir, cover and cook on Low for 8 hours.
3. Divide into bowls and serve hot.

Enjoy!

Nutrition: calories 200, fat 4, fiber 5, carbs 9, protein 12

Chinese Tofu and Veggies

Preparation time: 10 minutes
Cooking time: 4 hours
Servings: 4

Ingredients:

- 14 ounces extra firm tofu, pressed and cut into medium triangles
- Cooking spray
- 2 teaspoons ginger, grated
- 1 yellow onion, chopped
- 3 garlic cloves, minced
- 8 ounces tomato sauce
- ¼ cup hoisin sauce
- ¼ teaspoon coconut aminos
- 2 tablespoons rice wine vinegar
- 1 tablespoon soy sauce
- 1 tablespoon spicy mustard
- ¼ teaspoon red pepper, crushed
- 2 teaspoons molasses
- 2 tablespoons water
- A pinch of black pepper
- 3 broccoli stalks
- 1 green bell pepper, cut into squares
- 2 zucchinis, cubed

Directions:

1. Heat up a pan over medium high heat, add tofu pieces, brown them for a few minutes and transfer to your slow cooker.
2. Heat up the pan again over medium high heat, add ginger, onion, garlic and tomato sauce, stir, sauté for a few minutes and transfer to your slow cooker as well.
3. Add hoisin sauce, aminos, vinegar, soy sauce, mustard, red pepper, molasses, water and black pepper, stir gently, cover and cook on High for 3 hours.
4. Add zucchinis, bell pepper and broccoli, cover and cook on High for 1 more hour.
5. Divide between plates and serve right away.

Nutrition: calories 300, fat 4, fiber 8, carbs 14, protein 13

Wonderful Corn Chowder

Preparation time: 10 minutes
Cooking time: 8 hours and 30 minutes
Servings: 6

Ingredients:

- 2 cups yellow onion, chopped
- 2 tablespoons olive oil
- 1 red bell pepper, chopped
- 1 pound gold potatoes, cubed
- 1 teaspoon cumin, ground
- 4 cups corn kernels
- 4 cups veggie stock
- 1 cup almond milk
- A pinch of salt
- A pinch of cayenne pepper
- ½ teaspoon smoked paprika
- Chopped scallions for serving

Directions:

1. Heat up a pan with the oil over medium heat, add onion, stir and sauté for 5 minutes and then transfer to your slow cooker.
2. Add bell pepper, 1 cup corn, potatoes, paprika, cumin, salt and cayenne, stir, cover and cook on Low for 8 hours.
3. Blend this using an immersion blender and then mix with almond milk and the rest of the corn.
4. Stir chowder, cover and cook on Low for 30 minutes more.
5. Ladle into bowls and serve with chopped scallions on top.

Enjoy!

Nutrition: calories 200, fat 4, fiber 7, carbs 13, protein 16

Black Eyed Peas Stew

Preparation time: 10 minutes
Cooking time: 4 hours
Servings: 8

Ingredients:

- 3 celery stalks, chopped
- 2 carrots, sliced
- 1 yellow onion, chopped
- 1 sweet potato, cubed
- 1 green bell pepper, chopped
- 3 cups black-eyed peas, soaked for 8 hours and drained
- 1 cup tomato puree
- 4 cups veggie stock
- A pinch of salt
- Black pepper to the taste
- 1 chipotle chile, minced
- 1 teaspoon ancho chili powder
- 1 teaspoons sage, dried and crumbled
- 2 teaspoons cumin, ground
- Chopped coriander for serving

Directions:

1. Put celery in your slow cooker.
2. Add carrots, onion, potato, bell pepper, black-eyed peas, tomato puree, salt, pepper, chili powder, sage, chili, cumin and stock.
3. Stir, cover and cook on High for 4 hours.
4. Stir stew again, divide into bowls and serve with chopped coriander on top.

Enjoy!

Nutrition: calories 200, fat 4, fiber 7, carbs 9, protein 16

White Bean Cassoulet

Preparation time: 10 minutes
Cooking time: 6 hours
Servings: 4

Ingredients:

- 2 celery stalks, chopped
- 3 leeks, sliced
- 4 garlic cloves, minced
- 2 carrots, chopped
- 2 cups veggie stock
- 15 ounces canned tomatoes, chopped
- 1 bay leaf
- 1 tablespoon Italian seasoning
- 30 ounces canned white beans, drained
  For the breadcrumbs:
- Zest from 1 lemon, grated
- 1 garlic clove, minced
- 2 tablespoons olive oil
- 1 cup vegan bread crumbs
- ¼ cup parsley, chopped

Directions:

1. Heat up a pan with a splash of the veggie stock over medium heat, add celery and leeks, stir and cook for 2 minutes.
2. Add carrots and garlic, stir and cook for 1 minute more.
3. Add this to your slow cooker and mix with stock, tomatoes, bay leaf, Italian seasoning and beans.
4. Stir, cover and cook on Low for 6 hours.
5. Meanwhile, heat up a pan with the oil over medium high heat, add bread crumbs, lemon zest, 1 garlic clove and parsley, stir and toast for a couple of minutes.
6. Divide your white beans mix into bowls, sprinkle bread crumbs mix on top and serve.

Enjoy!

Nutrition: calories 223, fat 3, fiber 7, carbs 10, protein 7

Light Jackfruit Dish

Preparation time: 10 minutes
Cooking time: 6 hours
Servings: 4

Ingredients:

- 40 ounces green jackfruit in brine, drained
- ½ cup agave nectar
- ½ cup gluten free tamari sauce
- ¼ cup soy sauce
- 1 cup white wine
- 2 tablespoons ginger, grated
- 8 garlic cloves, minced
- 1 pear, cored and chopped
- 1 yellow onion, chopped
- ½ cup water
- 4 tablespoons sesame oil

Directions:

1. Put jackfruit in your slow cooker.
2. Add agave nectar, tamari sauce, soy sauce, wine, ginger, garlic, pear, onion, water and oil.
3. Stir well, cover and cook on Low for 6 hours.
4. Divide jackfruit mix into bowls and serve.

Enjoy!

Nutrition: calories 160, fat 4, fiber 1, carbs 10, protein 3

Veggie Curry

Preparation time: 10 minutes
Cooking time: 4 hours
Servings: 4

Ingredients:

- 1 tablespoon ginger, grated
- 14 ounces canned coconut milk
- Cooking spray
- 16 ounces firm tofu, pressed and cubed
- 1 cup veggie stock
- ¼ cup green curry paste
- ½ teaspoon turmeric
- 1 tablespoon coconut sugar
- 1 yellow onion, chopped
- 1 and ½ cup red bell pepper, chopped
- A pinch of salt
- ¾ cup peas
- 1 eggplant, chopped

Directions:

1. Put the coconut milk in your slow cooker.
2. Add ginger, stock, curry paste, turmeric, sugar, onion, bell pepper, salt, peas and eggplant pieces, stir, cover and cook on High for 4 hours.
3. Meanwhile, spray a pan with cooking spray and heat up over medium high heat.
4. Add tofu pieces and brown them for a few minutes on each side.
5. Divide tofu into bowls, add slowly cooked curry mix on top and serve.

Enjoy!

Nutrition: calories 200, fat 4, fiber 6, carbs 10, protein 9

Chickpeas Soup

Preparation time: 10 minutes
Cooking time: 4 hours
Servings: 6

Ingredients:

- 30 ounces canned chickpeas, drained
- 2 tablespoons mild curry powder
- 1 cup lentils, dry
- 1 sweet potato, cubed
- 15 ounces canned coconut milk
- 1 teaspoon ginger powder
- 1 teaspoon turmeric, ground
- A pinch of salt
- 6 cups veggie stock
- Black pepper to the taste

Directions:

1. Put chickpeas in your slow cooker.
2. Add lentils, sweet potato cubes, curry powder, ginger, turmeric, salt, pepper and stock.
3. Stir and then mix with coconut milk.
4. Stir again, cover and cook on High for 4 hours.
5. Ladle chickpeas soup into bowls and serve.

Enjoy!

Nutrition: calories 210, fat 4, fiber 6, carbs 9, protein 12

Hot and Delicious Soup

Preparation time: 10 minutes
Cooking time: 8 hours
Servings: 4

Ingredients:

- 8 ounces canned bamboo shoots, drained and chopped
- 10 ounces mushrooms, sliced
- 8 shiitake mushrooms, sliced
- 4 garlic cloves, minced
- 2 tablespoons ginger, grated
- 15 ounces extra firm tofu, pressed and cubed
- 2 tablespoons vegan bouillon
- 4 cups water
- 1 teaspoon sesame oil
- 2 tablespoons coconut aminos
- 1 teaspoon chili paste
- 1 and ½ cups peas
- 2 tablespoons rice wine vinegar

Directions:

1. Put the water in your slow cooker.
2. Add bamboo shoot, mushrooms, shiitake mushrooms, garlic, 1 tablespoon ginger, tofu, vegan bouillon, oil, aminos, chili paste, peas and vinegar.
3. Stir, cover and cook on Low for 8 hours.
4. Add the rest of the ginger, stir soup again, ladle into bowls and serve right away.

Enjoy!

Nutrition: calories 200, fat 5, fiber 5, carbs 16, protein 18

Delicious Eggplant Salad

Preparation time: 10 minutes
Cooking time: 8 hours
Servings: 4

Ingredients:

- 1 big eggplant, cut into quarters and then sliced
- 25 ounces canned plum tomatoes
- 2 red bell peppers, chopped
- 1 red onion, sliced
- 2 teaspoons cumin, ground
- A pinch of sea salt
- Black pepper to the taste
- 1 teaspoon smoked paprika
- Juice of 1 lemon

Directions:

1. In your slow cooker, mix eggplant pieces with tomatoes, bell peppers, onion, cumin, salt, pepper, paprika and lemon juice, stir, cover and cook on Low for 8 hours.
2. Stir again, divide into bowls and serve cold.

Enjoy!

Nutrition: calories 143, fat 2, fiber 3, carbs 7, protein 8

Tasty Black Beans Soup

Preparation time: 10 minutes
Cooking time: 6 hours
Servings: 6

Ingredients:

- 4 cups veggie stock
- 1 pound black beans, soaked overnight and drained
- 1 yellow onion, chopped
- 2 jalapenos, chopped
- 1 red bell pepper, chopped
- 1 cup tomatoes, chopped
- 4 garlic cloves, minced
- 1 tablespoon chili powder
- Black pepper to the taste
- 2 teaspoons cumin, ground
- A pinch of sea salt
- ½ teaspoon cayenne pepper
- 1 avocado, pitted, peeled and chopped
- ½ teaspoon sweet paprika

Directions:

1. Put the stock in your slow cooker.
2. Add beans, onion, jalapenos, bell pepper, tomatoes, garlic, chili powder, black pepper, salt, cumin, cayenne and paprika.
3. Stir, cover and cook on Low for 6 hours.
4. Blend soup using an immersion blender, ladle into bowls and serve with chopped avocado on top.

Enjoy!

Nutrition: calories 200, fat 2, fiber 3, carbs 7, protein 17

Rich Sweet Potato Soup

Preparation time: 10 minutes
Cooking time: 8 hours
Servings: 5

Ingredients:

- 5 cups veggie stock
- 2 celery stalks, chopped
- 3 sweet potatoes, chopped
- 1 cup yellow onion, chopped
- 2 garlic cloves, minced
- 1 cup rice milk
- 1 teaspoon tarragon, dried
- 2 cups baby spinach
- 8 tablespoons almonds, sliced
- A pinch of salt
- Black pepper to the taste

Directions:

1. Put the stock in your slow cooker.
2. Add celery, potatoes, onion, garlic, salt, pepper and tarragon.
3. Stir, cover and cook on Low for 8 hours.
4. Add rice milk and blend using an immersion blender.
5. Add almonds and spinach, stir, cover and leave aside for 20 minutes.
6. Ladle into bowls and serve.

Enjoy!

Nutrition: calories 230, fat 3, fiber 5, carbs 10, protein 18

Pumpkin Chili

Preparation time: 10 minutes
Cooking time: 8 hours
Servings: 6

Ingredients:

- 1 cup pumpkin, pureed
- 45 ounces canned black beans, drained
- 30 ounces canned tomatoes, chopped
- 1 yellow bell pepper, chopped
- 1 yellow onion, chopped
- ¼ teaspoon nutmeg, ground
- 1 teaspoon cinnamon powder
- 1 tablespoon chili powder
- 1 teaspoon cumin, ground
- 1/8 teaspoon cloves, ground
- A pinch of sea salt
- Black pepper to the taste

Directions:

1. Put pumpkin puree in your slow cooker.
2. Add black beans, tomatoes, onion, bell pepper, cumin, nutmeg, cinnamon, chili powder, cloves, salt and pepper, stir, cover and cook on Low for 8 hours.
3. Stir your chili again, divide into bowls and serve.

Enjoy!

Nutrition: calories 250, fat 5, fiber 9, carbs 12, protein 8

Crazy Cauliflower and Zucchini Surprise

Preparation time: 10 minutes
Cooking time: 3 hours and 30 minutes
Servings: 4

Ingredients:

- 1 cauliflower head, florets separated
- 2 garlic cloves, minced
- ¾ cup red onion, chopped
- 1 teaspoon basil, dried
- 2 teaspoons oregano flakes
- 28 ounces canned tomatoes, chopped
- ¼ teaspoon red pepper flakes
- ½ cup veggie stock
- 5 zucchinis, cut with a spiralizer
- A pinch of salt
- Black pepper to the taste

Directions:

1. Put cauliflower florets in your slow cooker.
2. Add garlic, onion, basil, oregano, tomatoes, stock, pepper flakes, salt and pepper, stir, cover and cook on High for 3 hours and 30 minutes.
3. Mash cauliflower mix a bit using a potato masher.
4. Divide zucchini noodles in bowls, top each with cauliflower mix and serve.

Enjoy!

Nutrition: calories 150, fat 2, fiber 3, carbs 6, protein 9

Quinoa and Veggies

Preparation time: 10 minutes
Cooking time: 4 hours
Servings: 4

Ingredients:

- 1 tablespoon olive oil
- 1 and ½ cups quinoa
- 3 cups veggie stock
- 1 yellow onion, chopped
- 1 carrot, chopped
- 1 sweet red pepper, chopped
- 1 cup green beans, chopped
- 2 garlic cloves, minced
- 1 teaspoon cilantro, chopped
- A pinch of salt
- Black pepper to the taste

Directions:

1. Put the stock in your slow cooker.
2. Add oil, quinoa, onion, carrot, sweet pepper, beans, cloves, salt and pepper, stir, cover and cook on Low for 4 hours.
3. Add cilantro, stir again, divide on plates and serve.

Enjoy!

Nutrition: calories 120, fat 2, fiber 3, carbs 6, protein 6

Spaghetti Squash Bowls

Preparation time: 10 minutes
Cooking time: 8 hours
Servings: 4

Ingredients:

- 5 pounds spaghetti squash, peeled
- 2 cups water
- 2 cups broccoli florets, steamed
- 1 tablespoon sesame seeds
- Chopped peanuts for serving
- ½ batch salad dressing
  For the salad dressing:
- 1 tablespoon palm sugar
- 1 tablespoon ginger, grated
- 3 tablespoons rice wine vinegar
- 3 tablespoons olive oil
- 2 tablespoons peanut butter
- 1 tablespoon soy sauce
- 3 garlic cloves, minced
- 1 teaspoon sesame oil
- ½ teaspoon sesame seeds

Directions:

1. In your blender, mix ginger with sugar, vinegar, oil, soy sauce, garlic, peanut butter, sesame oil and ½ teaspoon sesame seeds, pulse really well and leave aside.
2. Put the squash in your slow cooker, add the water, cover and cook on Low for 8 hours.
3. Leave squash to cool down, cut in halves, scrape flesh and transfer into a bowl.
4. Add broccoli florets, 1 tablespoon sesame seeds, chopped peanuts and the salad dressing.
5. Toss salad well and serve.

Enjoy!

Nutrition: calories 150, fat 4, fiber 7, carbs 17, protein 7

Amazing Curry

Preparation time: 10 minutes
Cooking time: 4 hours
Servings: 6

Ingredients:

- 3 cups sweet potatoes, cubed
- 2 cups broccoli florets
- 1 cup water
- 1 cup white onion, chopped
- 28 ounces canned tomatoes, chopped
- 15 ounces canned chickpeas, drained
- ¼ cup quinoa
- 29 ounces canned coconut milk
- 1 tablespoon garlic, minced
- 1 tablespoon ginger root, grated
- 1 tablespoon turmeric, ground
- 2 teaspoons vegan tamari sauce
- 1 teaspoon chili flakes

Directions:

1. Put the water in your slow cooker.
2. Add potatoes, broccoli, onion, tomatoes, chickpeas, quinoa, garlic, ginger, turmeric, chili flakes, tamari sauce and coconut milk.
3. Stir, cover and cook on High for 4 hours.
4. Stir your curry again, divide into bowls and serve.

Enjoy!

Nutrition: calories 400, fat 12, fiber 10, carbs 20, protein 10

Lentils and Lemon Soup

Preparation time: 10 minutes
Cooking time: 6 hours
Servings: 6

Ingredients:

- 1 yellow bell pepper, chopped
- 1 yellow onion, chopped
- 6 carrots, chopped
- 4 garlic cloves, minced
- A pinch of cayenne pepper
- 4 cups veggie stock
- 3 cups red lentils, dried
- 3 cups water
- A pinch of sea salt
- 1 tablespoon rosemary, chopped
- Zest and juice from 1 lemon

Directions:

1. Put the stock and water in your slow cooker.
2. Add bell pepper, onion, carrots, garlic, lentils, cayenne and salt.
3. Stir, cover and cook on Low for 6 hours.
4. Add rosemary, lemon zest and juice, stir, ladle into bowls and serve.

Enjoy!

Nutrition: calories 160, fat 2, fiber 5, carbs 8, protein 6

Autumn Veggie Mix

Preparation time: 10 minutes
Cooking time: 4 hours and 30 minutes
Servings: 6

Ingredients:

- 2 sweet potatoes, cubed
- 1 yellow onion, chopped
- 1 small cauliflower head, florets separated
- 14 ounces canned coconut milk
- 2 teaspoons sriracha sauce
- 3 tablespoons coconut aminos
- A pinch of salt
- 1 tablespoon palm sugar
- 3 tablespoons red curry paste
- 1 cup green peas
- 8 ounces white mushrooms, roughly chopped
- ½ cup cashews, toasted and chopped
- ¼ cup cilantro, chopped
- A few basil leaves, chopped for serving
- Brown rice for serving

Directions:

1. Put coconut milk in your slow cooker.
2. Add potatoes, onion, cauliflower florets, sriracha sauce, aminos, salt, curry paste and sugar, stir, cover and cook on Low for 4 hours.
3. Add mushrooms, peas, cilantro and basil, stir, cover and cook on Low for 30 minutes more.
4. Divide into bowls and serve with brown rice on the side and toasted cashews on top.

Enjoy!

Nutrition: calories 200, fat 3, fiber 5, carbs 15, protein 12

Special Veggie Stew

Preparation time: 10 minutes
Cooking time: 4 hours
Servings: 8

Ingredients:

- 1 yellow onion, chopped
- 1 teaspoon olive oil
- 2 red potatoes, chopped
- A pinch of salt and black pepper
- 1 tablespoon stevia
- 1 tablespoon curry powder
- 1 tablespoon ginger, grated
- 3 garlic cloves, minced
- 30 ounces canned chickpeas, drained
- 1 green bell pepper, chopped
- 2 cups veggie stock
- 1 red bell pepper, chopped
- 1 cauliflower head, florets separated
- 28 ounces canned tomatoes, chopped
- 1 cup coconut milk
- 10 ounces baby spinach

Directions:

1. In your slow cooker, mix oil with onion, potatoes, salt, pepper, stevia, curry powder, ginger, garlic, chickpeas, red and green bell pepper, stock, cauliflower, tomatoes, spinach and milk, stir, cover and cook on High for 4 minutes.
2. Stir your stew again, divide into bowls and serve.

Enjoy!

Nutrition: calories 319, fat 10, fiber 13, carbs 45, protein 14

Vegan Chickpeas Winter Mix

Preparation time: 10 minutes
Cooking time: 4 hours and 10 minutes
Servings: 6

Ingredients:

- 1 yellow onion, chopped
- 1 tablespoon ginger, grated
- 1 tablespoon olive oil
- 4 garlic cloves, minced
- A pinch of salt and black pepper
- 2 red Thai chilies, chopped
- ½ teaspoon turmeric powder
- 2 tablespoons garam masala
- 4 ounces tomato paste
- 2 cups veggie stock
- 6 ounces canned chickpeas, drained
- 2 tablespoons cilantro, chopped

Directions:

1. Heat up a pan with the oil over medium high heat, add ginger and onions, stir and cook for 4-5 minutes.
2. Add garlic, salt, pepper, Thai chilies, garam masala and turmeric, stir, cook for 2 minutes more and transfer everything to your slow cooker.
3. Add stock, chickpeas and tomato paste, stir, cover and cook on Low for 4 hours.
4. Add cilantro, stir, divide into bowls and serve.

Enjoy!

Nutrition: calories 211, fat 7, fiber 4, carbs 9, protein 7

Indian Lentils Mix

Preparation time: 10 minutes
Cooking time: 8 hours
Servings: 16

Ingredients:

- 4 garlic cloves, minced
- 4 cups brown lentils
- 2 yellow onions, chopped
- 1 tablespoon ginger, grated
- 4 tablespoons olive oil
- 1 tablespoon garam masala
- 4 tablespoons red curry paste
- 2 teaspoons stevia
- 1 and ½ teaspoons turmeric powder
- A pinch of salt and black pepper
- 45 ounces canned tomato puree
- ½ cup coconut milk
- 1 tablespoon cilantro, chopped

Directions:

1. In your slow cooker, mix lentils with onions, garlic, ginger, oil, curry paste, garam masala, turmeric, salt, pepper and stevia.
2. Also add tomato puree, stir, cover and cook on Low for 7 hour and 20 minutes.
3. Add coconut milk and cilantro, stir, cover and cook on Low for 40 minutes.
4. Divide into bowls and serve.

Enjoy!

Nutrition: calories 118, fat 5, fiber 4, carbs 18, protein 4

"Baked" Beans

Preparation time: 10 minutes
Cooking time: 12 hours
Servings: 6

Ingredients:

- 1 pound navy beans, soaked overnight and drained
- 1 cup maple syrup
- 1 cup vegan BBQ sauce
- 4 tablespoons stevia
- 1 cup water
- ¼ cup tomato paste
- ¼ cup mustard
- ¼ cup olive oil
- ¼ cup apple cider vinegar
- 2 tablespoons coconut aminos

Directions:

1. In your slow cooker, mix beans with maple syrup, BBQ sauce, stevia, water, tomato paste, mustard, oil, vinegar and aminos, stir, cover and cook on Low for 12 hours.
2. Divide into bowls and serve hot.

Enjoy!

Nutrition: calories 453, fat 7, fiber 12, carbs 40, protein 13

Squash Chili

Preparation time: 10 minutes
Cooking time: 6 hours
Servings: 8

Ingredients:

- 2 carrots, chopped
- 1 yellow onion, chopped
- 2 celery stalks, chopped
- 2 green apples, cored, peeled and chopped
- 4 garlic cloves, minced
- 2 cups butternut squash, peeled and cubed
- 6 ounces canned chickpeas, drained
- 6 ounces canned black beans, drained
- 7 ounces canned coconut milk
- 2 teaspoons chili powder
- 1 teaspoon oregano, dried
- 1 tablespoon cumin, ground
- 2 cups veggie stock
- 2 tablespoons tomato paste
- Salt and black pepper to the taste
- 1 tablespoon cilantro, chopped

Directions:

1. In your slow cooker, mix carrots with onion, celery, apples, garlic, squash, chickpeas, black beans, coconut milk, chili powder, oregano, cumin, stock, tomato paste, salt and pepper, stir, cover and cook on High for 6 hours.
2. Add cilantro, stir, divide into bowls and serve.

Enjoy!

Nutrition: calories 312, fat 6, fiber 8, carbs 12, protein 6

Rich Lentils Soup

Preparation time: 10 minutes
Cooking time: 2 hours and 30 minutes
Servings: 4

Ingredients:

- 2 teaspoons garlic, minced
- 1 tablespoon olive oil
- 1 yellow onion, chopped
- 1 teaspoon cumin, ground
- 1 teaspoon coriander seeds
- 1 teaspoon turmeric powder
- 1 teaspoon cinnamon powder
- ½ teaspoon garam masala
- 1 and ½ cups red lentils
- 4 cups veggie stock
- 14 ounces coconut milk
- 4 cups spinach
- Salt and black pepper to the taste

Directions:

1. In your slow cooker, mix garlic with oil, onion, cumin, coriander, turmeric, cinnamon, garam masala, lentils and stock, stir, cover and cook on High for 2 hours.
2. Add coconut, spinach, salt and pepper, stir and cook on High for 30 minutes more.
3. Ladle into bowls and serve.

Enjoy!

Nutrition: calories 271, fat 6, fiber 5, carbs 8, protein 4

Easy Lentils Mix

Preparation time: 10 minutes
Cooking time: 4 hours and 30 minutes
Servings: 6

Ingredients:

- 6 cups sweet potatoes, cubed
- 1 yellow onion, chopped
- 3 cups veggie stock
- 2 teaspoons coriander, ground
- 4 garlic cloves, minced
- 2 teaspoons chili powder
- 2 teaspoons garam masala
- 1 and ½ cups red lentils
- 8 ounces canned coconut milk
- 1 cup water
- A pinch of salt and black pepper to the taste

Directions:

1. In your slow cooker, mix potatoes with onion, stock, coriander, garlic, chili powder, garam masala, salt and pepper, stir, cover and cook on High for 3 hours.
2. Add lentils and water, stir, cover and cook on High for 1 hour and 30 minutes more.
3. Add coconut milk, more salt and pepper if needed, stir, cover, leave aside for a few minutes, divide between plates and serve.

Enjoy!

Nutrition: calories 334, fat 11, fiber 3, carbs 45, protein 11

Quinoa and Beans Chili

Preparation time: 10 minutes
Cooking time: 3 hours
Servings: 4

Ingredients:

- 15 ounces canned black beans, drained
- 2 and ¼ cups veggie stock
- ½ cup quinoa
- 14 ounces canned tomatoes, chopped
- ¼ cup red bell pepper, chopped
- 1 carrot, shredded
- ¼ cup green bell pepper, chopped
- 2 garlic cloves, minced
- ½ chili pepper, chopped
- 2 teaspoons chili powder
- 1 small yellow onion, chopped
- A pinch of salt and black pepper
- 1 teaspoon oregano, dried
- 1 teaspoon cumin, ground
- ½ cup corn

For the cashew cream:

- 4 tablespoons water
- ½ cup cashews, soaked overnight and drained
- A pinch of salt and black pepper
- A drizzle of white vinegar
- 1 teaspoon lime juice

Directions:

1. In your slow cooker, mix black beans with stock, quinoa, tomatoes, red and green bell pepper, carrot, garlic, chili, chili powder, onion, salt, pepper, oregano, cumin and corn, stir, cover and cook on High for 3 hours.
2. Meanwhile, in your blender, mix cashews with water, salt, pepper, vinegar and lime juice and pulse really well.
3. Divide chili into bowls, spread cashew cream on top and serve.

Enjoy!

Nutrition: calories 291, fat 7, fiber 4, carbs 28, protein 8

Potatoes and Spinach Mix

Preparation time: 10 minutes
Cooking time: 3 hours
Servings: 4

Ingredients:

- 1 pound potatoes, cubed
- 1 small onion, chopped
- 2 tablespoons water
- 1 tablespoon olive oil
- ½ teaspoon cumin, ground
- ½ teaspoon coriander, ground
- ½ teaspoon garam masala
- ½ teaspoon chili powder
- ½ pound spinach, torn
- Black pepper to the taste

Directions:

1. In your slow cooker, mix potatoes with onion, water, oil, cumin, coriander, garam masala, chili, spinach and black pepper, stir, cover and cook on High for 3 hours.
2. Divide into bowls and serve.

Enjoy!

Nutrition: calories 223, fat 4, fiber 7, carbs 12, protein 4

Rich White Bean Soup

Preparation time: 10 minutes
Cooking time: 4 hours
Servings: 6

Ingredients:
- 1 pounds navy beans, dried
- 1 yellow onion, chopped
- 2 quarts veggie stock
- Salt and black pepper to the taste
- 2 potatoes, cubed
- 1 pound carrots, sliced
- 1 cup sun-dried tomatoes, chopped
- 2 teaspoons dill, chopped
- 4 tablespoons parsley, chopped

Directions:
1. In your slow cooker, mix beans with onion, stock, salt, pepper, potatoes, carrots, tomatoes, dill and parsley, stir, cover and cook on High for 4 hours.
2. Ladle into bowls and serve.
Enjoy!

Nutrition: calories 271, fat 4, fiber 8, carbs 12, protein 4

Intense Tofu and Pineapple Mix

Preparation time: 10 minutes
Cooking time: 10 hours
Servings: 5

Ingredients:
- 2 pounds firm tofu, pressed and cut into medium rectangles
- 1 tablespoons sesame oil
- 3 tablespoons coconut aminos
- ½ cup veggie stock
- 1 cup pineapple juice
- ¼ cup rice vinegar
- 2 tablespoons stevia
- 1 tablespoon ginger, grated
- 3 garlic cloves, minced
- 6 pineapple rings

Directions:
1. In your slow cooker, mix tofu with sesame oil, coconut aminos, stock, pineapple juice, vinegar, stevia, ginger, garlic and pineapple rings, stir, cover and cook on Low for 10 hours.
2. Divide into bowls and serve.
Enjoy!

Nutrition: calories 231, fat 5, fiber 7, carbs 16, protein 4

Vegan Jambalaya

Preparation time: 10 minutes
Cooking time: 4 hours
Servings: 6

Ingredients:
- 1 green bell pepper, chopped
- 1 cup okra
- 1 small yellow onion, chopped
- 2 garlic cloves, minced
- 3 celery ribs, chopped
- 16 ounces canned tomatoes, chopped
- 1 and ½ cups veggie stock
- ½ teaspoon paprika
- A pinch of salt and black pepper

Directions:
1. In your slow cooker, mix bell pepper with okra, onion, garlic, celery, tomatoes, stock, paprika, salt and pepper, stir, cover and cook on Low for 4 hours.
2. Divide into bowls and serve.

Enjoy!

Nutrition: calories 132, fat 4, fiber 6, carbs 12, protein 4

Ratatouille

Preparation time: 10 minutes
Cooking time: 9 hours
Servings: 6

Ingredients:
- 2 yellow onions, chopped
- 1 eggplant, sliced
- 4 zucchinis, sliced
- 2 garlic cloves, minced
- 2 green bell peppers, cut into medium strips
- 6 ounces canned tomato paste
- 2 tomatoes, cut into medium wedges
- 1 teaspoon oregano, dried
- 1 teaspoon stevia
- 1 teaspoon basil, dried
- A pinch of salt and black pepper
- 2 tablespoons parsley, chopped
- ¼ cup olive oil
- A pinch of red pepper flakes, crushed

Directions:
1. In your slow cooker, mix oil with onions, eggplant, zucchinis, garlic, bell peppers, tomato paste, basil, oregano, salt and pepper, don't stir, cover and cook on Low for 9 hours.
2. Add pepper flakes and parsley, stir gently, divide between plates and serve.

Enjoy!

Nutrition: calories 139, fat 7, fiber 6, carbs 17, protein 4

Pinto Beans and Tasty Rice

Preparation time: 10 minutes
Cooking time: 3 hours
Servings: 6

Ingredients:
- 1 pound pinto beans, dried
- 1/3 cup picanto sauce
- A pinch of salt and black pepper
- 1 tablespoon garlic, minced
- 1 teaspoon garlic powder
- ½ teaspoon cumin, ground
- 1 tablespoon chili powder
- 3 bay leaves
- ½ teaspoon oregano, dried
- 1 cup white rice, cooked

Directions:
1. In your slow cooker, mix pinto beans with picanto sauce, salt, pepper, garlic, garlic powder, cumin, chili powder, bay leaves and oregano, stir, cover and cook on High for 3 hours.
2. Divide rice on plates, add pinto beans mix on top and serve.

Enjoy!

Nutrition: calories 381, fat 7, fiber 12, carbs 35, protein 10

Black Beans, Rice and Mango

Preparation time: 10 minutes
Cooking time: 6 hours and 20 minutes
Servings: 6

Ingredients:
- 1 yellow onion, chopped
- 1 tablespoon olive oil
- 1 red bell pepper, chopped
- 1 jalapeno, chopped
- 2 garlic cloves, minced
- 1 teaspoon ginger, grated
- ½ teaspoon cumin
- ½ teaspoon allspice, ground
- ½ teaspoon oregano, dried
- 30 ounces canned black beans, drained
- ½ teaspoon stevia
- 1 cup water
- A pinch of salt and black pepper
- 3 cups brown rice, cooked
- 2 mangoes, peeled and chopped

Directions:
1. Heat up a pan with the oil over medium high heat, add onion, stir and cook for 3-4 minutes,
2. Add garlic, ginger and jalapeno, stir, cook for 3 minutes more and transfer to your slow cooker.
3. Add red bell pepper, cumin, allspice, oregano, black beans, stevia, water, salt and pepper, stir, cover and cook on Low for 6 hours.
4. Add rice and mangoes, stir, cover and cook on Low for 10 minutes more.
5. Divide between plates and serve.

Enjoy!

Nutrition: calories 490, fat 6, fiber 20, carbs 80, protein 17

Spinach Soup

Preparation time: 10 minutes
Cooking time: 10 hours
Servings: 8

Ingredients:

- 10 ounces baby spinach
- 2 celery ribs, chopped
- 2 carrots, chopped
- 1 garlic clove, minced
- 1 yellow onion, chopped
- 4 cups veggie stock
- 28 ounces tomatoes, chopped
- 2 bay leaves
- 1 teaspoon oregano, dried
- 1 tablespoon basil, chopped
- ½ teaspoon red pepper flakes, crushed

Directions:

1. In your slow cooker, mix spinach with celery, carrots, garlic, onion, stock, tomatoes, bay leaves, oregano, basil, red pepper flakes, stir, cover and cook on Low for 10 hours.
2. Ladle into bowls and serve.

Enjoy!

Nutrition: calories 100, fat 4, fiber 4, carbs 9, protein 3

Split Pea Soup

Preparation time: 10 minutes
Cooking time: 6 hours
Servings: 6

Ingredients:

- 2 cups split peas, rinsed
- 6 cups water
- 1 celery stalk, chopped
- 1 carrot, chopped
- A pinch of salt and black pepper
- ¼ teaspoon thyme, dried
- 1 yellow onion, chopped
- A pinch of red pepper, crushed
- 1 bay leaf

Directions:

1. In your slow cooker, mix peas with water, celery, carrot, salt, pepper, thyme, onion, bay leaf and red pepper, stir, cover and cook on Low for 6 hours.
2. Discard bay leaf, add more salt and pepper if needed, blend using an immersion blender, ladle into bowls and serve.

Enjoy!

Nutrition: calories 178, fat 5, fiber 14, carbs 32, protein 12

Yam Stew

Preparation time: 10 minutes
Cooking time: 8 hours
Servings: 8

Ingredients:

- 1 yellow onion, chopped
- ½ cup red beans, dried
- 2 red bell peppers, chopped
- 2 tablespoons ginger, grated
- 4 garlic cloves, minced
- 2 pounds yams, peeled and cubed
- 3 cups veggie stock
- 14 ounces canned tomatoes, chopped
- 2 jalapeno peppers, chopped
- Salt and black pepper to the taste
- ½ teaspoon cumin, ground
- ½ teaspoon coriander, ground
- ¼ teaspoon cinnamon powder
- ¼ cup peanut butter
- ¼ cup peanuts, roasted and chopped
- Juice of ½ lime

Directions:

1. In your slow cooker, mix onion with red beans, red bell peppers, ginger, garlic, yams, stock, tomatoes, jalapenos, salt, pepper, cumin, coriander and cinnamon, stir, cover and cook on Low for 8 hours.
2. Add peanut butter and stir until it melts.
3. Divide into bowls, divide peanuts on top and drizzle lime juice on top.

Enjoy!

Nutrition: calories 259, fat 8, fiber 7, carbs 42, protein 8

Special Minestrone Soup

Preparation time: 10 minutes
Cooking time: 4 hours
Servings: 8

Ingredients:

- 2 zucchinis, chopped
- 3 carrots, chopped
- 1 yellow onion, chopped
- A handful green beans
- 3 celery stalks, chopped
- 4 garlic cloves, minced
- 10 ounces canned garbanzo beans
- 1 pound lentils, cooked
- 4 cups veggie stock
- 28 ounces canned tomatoes, chopped
- 1 teaspoon curry powder
- ½ teaspoon garam masala
- ½ teaspoon cumin, ground
- A pinch of salt and black pepper

Directions:

1. In your slow cooker, mix zucchinis with carrots, onion, green beans, celery, garlic, garbanzo beans, lentils, stock, tomatoes, salt, pepper, cumin, curry powder and garam masala, stir, cover and cook on High for 4 hours.
2. Ladle soup into bowls and serve.

Enjoy!

Nutrition: calories 193, fat 12, fiber 7, carbs 34, protein 10

Green Chili Soup

Preparation time: 10 minutes
Cooking time: 6 hours
Servings: 6

Ingredients:
- 2 jalapeno chilies, chopped
- 1 cup yellow onion, chopped
- 1 tablespoon olive oil
- 4 poblano chilies, chopped
- 4 Anaheim chilies, chopped
- 3 cups corn
- 10 epazote leaves, shredded
- 6 cups water
- ½ bunch cilantro, chopped
- Salt and black pepper to the taste

Directions:
1. In your slow cooker, mix jalapenos with onion, oil, poblano chilies, Anaheim chilies, corn and water, stir, cover and cook on Low for 6 hours.
2. Add cilantro, epazote leaves, salt and pepper, stir, transfer to your blender, pulse well, divide into bowls and serve.

Enjoy!

Nutrition: calories 179, fat 5, fiber 5, carbs 33, protein 5

Caribbean Dish

Preparation time: 10 minutes
Cooking time: 4 hours and 40 minutes
Servings: 6

Ingredients:
- 2 tablespoons coconut oil
- 28 ounces canned black beans
- 2 yellow onions, chopped
- 4 garlic cloves, minced
- 1 green bell pepper, chopped
- 1 teaspoon thyme, dried
- 2 teaspoons chili flakes
- 1 tablespoon stevia
- 4 potatoes, cut into medium cubes
- A pinch of salt and cayenne pepper
- 28 ounces canned tomatoes, chopped
- 1 cup veggie stock
- 14 ounces coconut milk

Directions:
1. Heat up a pan with the oil over medium high heat, add onion, garlic, stevia, bell pepper, thyme, chili flakes, salt and cayenne, stir and cook for 3-4 minutes.
2. Add stock, stir, cook for 30 seconds more and transfer to your slow cooker.
3. Add beans, tomatoes and potatoes to your slow cooker as well, cover and cook on High for 4 hours.
4. Add coconut milk, stir, cover pot and cook on Low for 30 minutes more.
5. Divide mix between plates and serve.

Enjoy!

Nutrition: 475, fat 16, fiber 15, carbs 76, protein 14

Mediterranean Stew

Preparation time: 10 minutes
Cooking time: 7 hours
Servings: 10

Ingredients:
- 2 cups eggplant, cubed
- 1 butternut squash, peeled and cubed
- 2 cups zucchini, cubed
- 10 ounces tomato sauce
- 1 carrot, sliced
- 1 yellow onion, chopped
- ½ cup veggie stock
- 10 ounces okra
- 1/3 cup raisins
- 2 garlic cloves, minced
- ½ teaspoon turmeric powder
- ½ teaspoon cumin, ground
- ½ teaspoon red pepper flakes, crushed
- ¼ teaspoon sweet paprika
- ¼ teaspoon cinnamon powder

Directions:
1. In your slow cooker, mix eggplant with squash, zucchini, tomato sauce, carrot, onion, okra, garlic, stock, raisins, turmeric, cumin, pepper flakes, paprika and cinnamon, stir, cover and cook on Low for 7 hours.
2. Stir your stew one more time, divide into bowls and serve.

Enjoy!

Nutrition: calories 100, fat 3, fiber 4, carbs 24, protein 3

Chickpeas Delight

Preparation time: 10 minutes
Cooking time: 12 hours
Servings: 14

Ingredients:
- 6 cups chickpeas
- 11 cups water
- 1 yellow onion, chopped
- 1 tablespoon ginger, grated
- 20 garlic cloves, minced
- 8 Thai peppers, chopped
- 2 tablespoons cumin, ground
- 2 tablespoons coriander, ground
- 1 tablespoons red chili powder
- 2 tablespoons garam masala
- 2 tablespoons vegan tamarind paste
- Juice of ½ lemon

Directions:
1. In your slow cooker, mix chickpeas with water, stir, cover and cook on Low for 10 hours.
2. In your blender, mix onion with ginger, garlic, Thai peppers, cumin, coriander, chili powder, garam masala, tamarind paste and lemon juice and pulse well.
3. Add this mix to slow cooker, toss, cover and cook on Low for 2 hours more.
4. Divide into bowls and serve.

Enjoy!

Nutrition: calories 355, fat 5, fiber 14, carbs 56, protein 17

Mexican Quinoa Dish

Preparation time: 10 minutes
Cooking time: 4 hours
Servings: 4

Ingredients:

- 15 ounces canned black beans, drained
- 30 ounces canned red enchilada sauce
- 15 ounces canned corn, drained
- 15 ounces canned tomatoes and green chilies, chopped
- 1 cup quinoa
- ½ cup water
- Salt and black pepper to the taste
- 1 cup vegan cheese, shredded

Directions:

1. In your slow cooker, mix black beans with corn, enchilada sauce, tomatoes and chilies, quinoa, water, salt and pepper and toss.
2. Sprinkle vegan cheese on top, cover and cook on High for 4 hours.
3. Divide into bowls and serve hot.

Enjoy!

Nutrition: calories 400, fat 3, fiber 14, carbs 32, protein 6

Sweet Potato Soup

Preparation time: 10 minutes
Cooking time: 5 hours and 20 minutes
Servings: 6

Ingredients:

- 5 cups veggie stock
- 3 sweet potatoes, peeled and chopped
- 2 celery stalks, chopped
- 1 cup yellow onion, chopped
- 1 cup almond milk
- 1 teaspoon tarragon, dried
- 2 garlic cloves, minced
- 2 cups baby spinach
- 8 tablespoons almonds, sliced
- A pinch of salt and black pepper

Directions:

1. In your slow cooker, mix stock with potatoes, celery, onion, almond milk, tarragon, garlic, salt and pepper, stir, cover and cook on High for 5 hours.
2. Blend soup using an immersion blender, add more salt and pepper if needed, also add spinach and almonds, toss, cover and leave aside for 20 minutes.
3. Divide soup into bowls and serve.

Enjoy!

Nutrition: calories 311, fat 5, fiber 4, carbs 12, protein 5

White Beans Stew

Preparation time: 10 minutes
Cooking time: 4 hours
Servings: 10

Ingredients:

- 2 pounds white beans
- 3 celery stalks, chopped
- 2 carrots, chopped
- 1 bay leaf
- 1 yellow onion, chopped
- 3 garlic cloves, minced
- 1 teaspoon rosemary, dried
- 1 teaspoon oregano, dried
- 1 teaspoon thyme, dried
- 10 cups water
- Salt and black pepper to the taste
- 28 ounces canned tomatoes, chopped
- 6 cups chard, chopped

Directions:

1. In your slow cooker, mix white beans with celery, carrots, bay leaf, onion, garlic, rosemary, oregano, thyme, water, salt, pepper, tomatoes and chard, toss, cover and cook on High for 4 hours.
2. Stir your stew one more time, divide into bowls and serve.

Enjoy!

Nutrition: calories 341, fat 8, fiber 12, carbs 20, protein 6

Spaghetti Squash Bowls

Preparation time: 10 minutes
Cooking time: 8 hours
Servings: 5

Ingredients:

- 1 spaghetti squash, halved
- 2 cups water
- 2 cups broccoli florets
- 1 tablespoon sesame seeds

For the salad dressing:

- 1 and ½ tablespoon stevia
- 3 tablespoons wine vinegar
- 3 tablespoons olive oil
- 1 tablespoon coconut aminos
- 1 tablespoon ginger, grated
- 2 garlic cloves, minced
- 1 teaspoon sesame oil

Directions:

1. In your blender, mix stevia with vinegar, oil, aminos, ginger, garlic and sesame oil, pulse really well and leave aside for now.
2. In your slow cooker, mix spaghetti squash with water, cover and cook on Low for 8 hours.
3. Transfer squash to a cutting board, cool it down, scrape flesh and transfer to a bowl.
4. Add broccoli and sesame seeds and toss.
5. Add salad dressing, toss well and serve.

Enjoy!

Nutrition: calories 150, fat 4, fiber 6, carbs 26, protein 6

Italian Cauliflower Mix

Preparation time: 10 minutes
Cooking time: 3 hours and 30 minutes
Servings: 4

Ingredients:
- 1 cauliflower head, florets separated
- 2 teaspoons oregano, dried
- 1 cup red onion, chopped
- 2 garlic cloves, minced
- 1 teaspoon basil, dried
- 28 ounces canned tomatoes, chopped
- ½ cup veggie stock
- Salt and black pepper to the taste
- A pinch of red pepper flakes
- 6 zucchinis, cut with a spiralizer

Directions:
1. In your slow cooker, mix cauliflower with oregano, onion, garlic, basil, tomatoes, stock, pepper flakes, salt and pepper, stir, cover and cook on High for 3 hours and 30 minutes.
2. Divide zucchini noodles into bowls, divide cauliflower mix on top, toss a bit and serve.

Enjoy!

Nutrition: calories 251, fat 5, fiber 7, carbs 10, protein 4

Mushroom Delight

Preparation time: 10 minutes
Cooking time: 4 hours
Servings: 2

Ingredients:
- 1 pound mushrooms, halved
- 1 yellow onion, chopped
- 3 garlic cloves, minced
- 1 cup veggie stock
- 1 tablespoon coconut cream
- 2 teaspoons smoked paprika
- Salt and black pepper to the taste
- 4 tablespoons parsley, chopped

Directions:
1. In your slow cooker, mix mushrooms with garlic, onion, stock and paprika, stir, cover and cook on High for 4 hours.
2. Add parsley, coconut cream, salt and pepper, toss, divide into bowls and serve.

Enjoy!

Nutrition: calories 300, fat 6, fiber 12, carbs 16, protein 6

Quinoa And Veggie Mix

Preparation time: 10 minutes
Cooking time: 4 hours
Servings: 4

Ingredients:

- 3 cups veggie stock
- 1 and ½ cups quinoa
- 1 tablespoon olive oil
- 1 yellow onion, chopped
- 1 sweet red pepper, chopped
- 1 cup green beans, chopped
- 1 carrot, chopped
- 3 garlic cloves, minced
- 1 teaspoon basil, chopped
- Salt and black pepper to the taste

Directions:

1. In your slow cooker, mix stock with quinoa, oil, onion, red pepper, green beans, carrot, garlic, basil, salt and pepper, stir, cover and cook on Low for 4 hours.
2. Divide into bowls and serve.

Enjoy!

Nutrition: calories 312, fat 6, fiber 12, carbs 18, protein 5

Bulgur Chili

Preparation time: 10 minutes
Cooking time: 8 hours
Servings: 4

Ingredients:

- 2 cups white mushrooms, sliced
- ¾ cup bulgur, soaked in 1 cup hot water for 15 minutes and drained
- 2 cups yellow onion, chopped
- ½ cup red bell pepper, chopped
- 1 cup veggie stock
- 2 garlic cloves, minced
- 1 cup strong brewed coffee
- 14 ounces canned kidney beans, drained
- 14 ounces canned pinto beans, drained
- 2 tablespoons stevia
- 2 tablespoons chili powder
- 1 tablespoon cocoa powder
- 1 teaspoon oregano, dried
- 2 teaspoons cumin, ground
- 1 bay leaf
- Salt and black pepper to the taste

Directions:

1. In your slow cooker, mix mushrooms with bulgur, onion, bell pepper, stock, garlic, coffee, kidney and pinto beans, stevia, chili powder, cocoa, oregano, cumin, bay leaf, salt and pepper, stir gently, cover and cook on Low for 12 hours.
2. Discard bay leaf, divide chili into bowls and serve.

Enjoy!

Nutrition: calories 351, fat 4, fiber 6, carbs 20, protein 4

Cauliflower Chili

Preparation time: 10 minutes
Cooking time: 8 hours
Servings: 4

Ingredients:
- 30 ounces canned cannellini beans, drained
- 4 cups cauliflower florets
- 1 yellow onion, chopped
- 28 ounces canned tomatoes and juice
- 4 ounces canned roasted green chilies, chopped
- ½ cup hot sauce
- 1 tablespoon stevia
- 2 teaspoons cumin, ground
- 1 tablespoon chili powder
- A pinch of salt and cayenne pepper

Directions:
1. In your slow cooker, mix cannellini beans with cauliflower, onion, tomatoes and juice, roasted green chilies, hot sauce, stevia, cumin, chili powder, salt and cayenne pepper, stir, cover and cook on Low for 8 hours.
2. Divide into bowls and serve hot.

Enjoy!

Nutrition: calories 314, fat 6, fiber 6, carbs 29, protein 5

Quinoa Chili

Preparation time: 10 minutes
Cooking time: 6 hours
Servings: 6

Ingredients:
- 2 cups veggie stock
- ½ cup quinoa
- 30 ounces canned black beans, drained
- 28 ounces canned tomatoes, chopped
- 1 green bell pepper, chopped
- 1 yellow onion, chopped
- 2 sweet potatoes, cubed
- 1 tablespoon chili powder
- 2 tablespoons cocoa powder
- 2 teaspoons cumin, ground
- Salt and black pepper to the taste
- ¼ teaspoon smoked paprika

Directions:
1. In your slow cooker, mix stock with quinoa, black beans, tomatoes, bell pepper, onion, sweet potatoes, chili powder, cocoa, cumin, paprika, salt and pepper, stir, cover and cook on High for 6 hours.
2. Divide into bowls and serve hot.

Enjoy!

Nutrition: calories 342, fat 6, fiber 7, carbs 18, protein 4

Pumpkin Chili

Preparation time: 10 minutes
Cooking time: 5 hours
Servings: 6

Ingredients:

- 1 cup pumpkin puree
- 30 ounces canned kidney beans, drained
- 30 ounces canned roasted tomatoes, chopped
- 2 cups water
- 1 cup red lentils, dried
- 1 cup yellow onion, chopped
- 1 jalapeno pepper, chopped
- 1 tablespoon chili powder
- 1 tablespoon cocoa powder
- ½ teaspoon cinnamon powder
- 2 teaspoons cumin, ground
- A pinch of cloves, ground
- Salt and black pepper to the taste
- 2 tomatoes, chopped

Directions:

1. In your slow cooker, mix pumpkin puree with kidney beans, roasted tomatoes, water, lentils, onion, jalapeno, chili powder, cocoa, cinnamon, cumin, cloves, salt and pepper, stir, cover and cook on High for 5 hours.
2. Divide into bowls, top with chopped tomatoes and serve hot.

Enjoy!

Nutrition: calories 266, fat 6, fiber 4, carbs 12, protein 4

3 Bean Chili

Preparation time: 10 minutes
Cooking time: 8 hours
Servings: 6

Ingredients:

- 15 ounces canned kidney beans, drained
- 30 ounces canned chili beans in sauce
- 15 ounces canned black beans, drained
- 2 green bell peppers, chopped
- 30 ounces canned tomatoes, crushed
- 2 tablespoons chili powder
- 2 yellow onions, chopped
- 2 garlic cloves, minced
- 1 teaspoon oregano, dried
- 1 tablespoon cumin, ground
- Salt and black pepper to the taste

Directions:

1. In your slow cooker, mix kidney beans with chili beans, black beans, bell peppers, tomatoes, chili powder, onion, garlic, oregano, cumin, salt and pepper, stir, cover and cook on Low for 8 hours.
2. Divide into bowls and serve.

Enjoy!

Nutrition: calories 314, fat 6, fiber 5, carbs 14, protein 4

Root Vegetable Chili

Preparation time: 10 minutes
Cooking time: 6 hours
Servings: 12

Ingredients:

- 2 cups turnips, cubed
- 2 cups rutabagas, cubed
- 2 cups sweet potatoes, cubed
- 2 cups parsnips, cubed
- 1 cup beets, cubed
- 1 cup carrots, cubed
- 1 and ½ cups yellow onion, chopped
- 8 ounces tempeh, rinsed and cubed
- 28 ounces canned tomatoes, chopped
- 1 cup veggie stock
- 15 ounces canned black beans, drained
- 15 ounces canned kidney beans, drained
- Salt and black pepper to the taste
- 1 teaspoon cumin, ground
- 1 teaspoon chili powder, ground
- A pinch of cayenne pepper
- ½ teaspoon nutmeg, ground
- ½ teaspoon sweet paprika
- ½ cup parsley, chopped

Directions:

1. In your slow cooker, mix turnips with rutabagas, sweet potatoes, parsnips, beets, carrots, onion, tempeh, tomatoes, stock, black and kidney beans, salt, pepper, cumin, chili powder, cayenne, nutmeg and paprika, stir, cover and cook on Low for 6 hours.
2. Add parsley, stir, divide into bowls and serve.

Enjoy!

Nutrition: calories 311, fat 6, fiber 6, carbs 16, protein 6

Brown Rice Soup

Preparation time: 10 minutes
Cooking time: 8 hours
Servings: 6

Ingredients:

- 70 ounces canned black beans, drained
- 1 cup yellow onion, chopped
- 1 tablespoon olive oil
- 2 carrots, chopped
- 1 jalapeno pepper, chopped
- 3 garlic cloves, minced
- 1 teaspoon cumin, ground
- 1 teaspoon chili powder
- 1 teaspoon oregano, dried
- Salt and black pepper to the taste
- 2 tablespoons tomato paste
- 4 cups veggie stock
- A splash of Tabasco sauce
- 2 cups brown rice, already cooked
- 1 tablespoon cilantro, chopped

Directions:

1. Drizzle the olive oil on the bottom of your slow cooker.
2. Add black beans, onion, carrots, jalapeno, garlic, cumin, chili, oregano, tomato paste, stock, Tabasco, salt, pepper and rice, stir, cover and cook on Low for 8 hours.
3. Add cilantro, stir, ladle into bowls and serve.

Enjoy!

Nutrition: calories 314, fat 5, fiber 8, carbs 18, protein 4

Butternut Squash Soup

Preparation time: 10 minutes
Cooking time: 8 hours
Servings: 6

Ingredients:

- 3 pounds butternut squash, peeled and cubed
- 1 yellow onion, chopped
- 4 cups veggie stock
- 14 ounces coconut milk
- Salt and black pepper to the taste
- 3 tablespoons red curry paste
- 1 tablespoon cilantro, chopped

Directions:

1. In your slow cooker, mix squash with onion, stock, milk, curry paste, salt and pepper, stir, cover and cook on Low for 8 hours
2. Blend using an immersion blender, ladle soup into bowls, sprinkle cilantro on top and serve.

Enjoy!

Nutrition: calories 237, fat 5, fiber 6, carbs 19, protein 6

Green Beans Soup

Preparation time: 10 minutes
Cooking time: 4 hours
Servings: 4

Ingredients:

- 1 pound green beans
- 1 yellow onion, chopped
- 4 carrots, chopped
- 4 garlic cloves, minced
- 1 tablespoon thyme, chopped
- 7 cups veggie stock
- Salt and black pepper to the taste

Directions:

1. In your slow cooker, mix green beans with onion, carrots, garlic, stock, salt and pepper, stir, cover and cook on High for 4 hours.
2. Add thyme, stir, ladle soup into bowls and serve.

Enjoy!

Nutrition: calories 231, fat 4, fiber 6, carbs 7, protein 5

Rich Chickpeas And Lentils Soup

Preparation time: 10 minutes
Cooking time: 5 hours
Servings: 6

Ingredients:
- 1 yellow onion, chopped
- 1 tablespoon olive oil
- 1 tablespoon garlic, minced
- 1 teaspoons sweet paprika
- 1 teaspoon smoked paprika
- Salt and black pepper to the taste
- 1 cup red lentils
- 15 ounces canned chickpeas, drained
- 4 cups veggie stock
- 29 ounces canned tomatoes and juice

Directions:
1. In your slow cooker, mix onion with oil, garlic, sweet and smoked paprika, salt, pepper, lentils, chickpeas, stock and tomatoes, stir, cover and cook on High for 5 hours.
2. Ladle into bowls and serve hot.

Enjoy!

Nutrition: calories 341, fat 5, fiber 8, carbs 19, protein 3

Chard And Sweet Potato Soup

Preparation time: 10 minutes
Cooking time: 8 hours
Servings: 6

Ingredients:
- 1 yellow onion, chopped
- 1 tablespoon olive oil
- 1 carrot, chopped
- 1 celery stalk, chopped
- 1 bunch Swiss chard, leaves torn
- 2 garlic cloves, minced
- 4 sweet potatoes, cubed
- 1 cup brown lentils, dried
- 6 cups veggie stock
- 1 tablespoon coconut aminos
- Salt and black pepper to the taste

Directions:
1. In your slow cooker, mix oil with onion, carrot, celery, chard, garlic, potatoes, lentils, stock, salt, pepper and aminos, stir, cover and cook on Low for 8 hours.
2. Ladle soup into bowls and serve right away.

Enjoy!

Nutrition: calories 312, fat 5, fiber 7, carbs 10, protein 5

Chinese Soup And Ginger Sauce

Preparation time: 10 minutes
Cooking time: 8 hours
Servings: 6

Ingredients:

- 2 celery stalks, chopped
- 1 yellow onion, chopped
- 1 cup carrot, chopped
- 8 ounces water chestnuts
- 8 ounces canned bamboo shoots, drained
- 2 teaspoons garlic, minced
- 2 teaspoons ginger paste
- ½ teaspoon red pepper flakes
- 3 tablespoons coconut aminos
- 1-quart veggie stock
- 2 bunches bok choy, chopped
- 5 ounces white mushrooms, sliced
- 8 ounces tofu, drained and cubed
- 1 ounce snow peas, cut into small pieces
- 6 scallions, chopped

For the ginger sauce:

- 1 teaspoon sesame oil
- 2 tablespoons ginger paste
- 2 tablespoons agave syrup
- 2 tablespoon coconut aminos

Directions:

1. In your slow cooker, mix onion with carrot, celery, chestnuts, bamboo shoots, garlic paste, 2 teaspoons ginger paste, pepper flakes, 3 tablespoons coconut aminos, stock, bok choy, mushrooms, tofu, snow peas and scallions, stir, cover and cook on Low for 8 hours.
2. In a bowl, mix 2 tablespoons ginger paste with agave syrup, 2 tablespoons coconut aminos and sesame oil and whisk well.
3. Ladle Chinese soup into bowls, add ginger sauce on top and serve.

Enjoy!

Nutrition: calories 300, fat 4, fiber 6, carbs 19, protein 4

Corn Cream Soup

Preparation time: 10 minutes
Cooking time: 8 hours and 10 minutes
Servings: 6

Ingredients:

- 1 yellow onion, chopped
- 2 tablespoons olive oil
- 1 red bell pepper, chopped
- 3 cups gold potatoes, chopped
- 4 cups corn kernels
- 4 cups veggie stock
- ½ teaspoon smoked paprika
- 1 teaspoon cumin, ground
- Salt and black pepper to the taste
- 1 cup almond milk
- 2 scallions, chopped

Directions:

1. Heat up a pan with the oil over medium high heat, add onion, stir and cook for 5-6 minutes.
2. Transfer this to your slow cooker, add bell pepper, potatoes, 3 cups corn, stock, paprika, cumin, salt and pepper, stir, cover and cook on Low for 7 hours and 30 minutes.
3. Blend soup using an immersion blender, add almond milk and blend again.
4. Add the rest of the corn, cover pot and cook on Low for 30 minutes more.
5. Ladle soup into bowls, sprinkle scallions on top and serve.

Enjoy!

Nutrition: calories 312, fat 4, fiber 6, carbs 12, protein 4

Veggie Medley

Preparation time: 10 minutes
Cooking time: 4 hours
Servings: 6

Ingredients:
- 1 tablespoon ginger, grated
- 3 garlic cloves, minced
- 1 date, pitted and chopped
- 1 and ½ teaspoon coriander, ground
- ½ teaspoon dry mustard
- 1 and ¼ teaspoon cumin, ground
- A pinch of salt and black pepper
- ½ teaspoon turmeric powder
- 1 tablespoon white wine vinegar
- ¼ teaspoon cardamom, ground
- 2 carrots, chopped
- 1 yellow onion, chopped
- 4 cups cauliflower florets
- 1 and ½ cups kidney beans, cooked
- 2 zucchinis, chopped
- 6 ounces tomato paste
- 1 green bell pepper, chopped
- 1 cup green peas

Directions:
1. In your slow cooker, mix ginger with garlic, date, coriander, dry mustard, cumin, salt, pepper, turmeric, vinegar, cardamom, carrots, onion, cauliflower, kidney beans, zucchinis, tomato paste, bell pepper and peas, stir, cover and cook on High for 4 hours.
2. Divide into bowls and serve hot.

Enjoy!

Nutrition: calories 165, fat 2, fiber 10, carbs 32, protein 9

Lentils Curry

Preparation time: 10 minutes
Cooking time: 6 hours
Servings: 8

Ingredients:
- 10 ounces spinach
- 2 cups red lentils
- 1 tablespoon garlic, minced
- 15 ounces canned tomatoes, chopped
- 2 cups cauliflower florets
- 1 teaspoon ginger, grated
- 1 yellow onion, chopped
- 4 cups veggie stock
- 2 tablespoons curry paste
- ½ teaspoon cumin, ground
- ½ teaspoon coriander, ground
- 2 teaspoons stevia
- A pinch of salt and black pepper
- ¼ cup cilantro, chopped
- 1 tablespoon lime juice

Directions:
1. In your slow cooker, mix spinach with lentils, garlic, tomatoes, cauliflower, ginger, onion, stock, curry paste, cumin, coriander, stevia, salt, pepper and lime juice, stir, cover and cook on Low for 6 hours.
2. Add cilantro, stir, divide into bowls and serve.

Enjoy!

Nutrition: calories 105, fat 1, fiber 7, carbs 22, protein 7

Lentils Dal

Preparation time: 10 minutes
Cooking time: 5 hours
Servings: 12

Ingredients:

- 6 cups water
- 3 cups red lentils
- 28 ounces canned tomatoes, chopped
- 1 yellow onion, chopped
- 4 garlic cloves, minced
- 1 tablespoon turmeric powder
- 2 tablespoons ginger, grated
- 3 cardamom pods
- 1 bay leaf
- 2 teaspoons mustard seeds
- 2 teaspoons onion seeds
- 2 teaspoons fenugreek seeds
- 1 teaspoon fennel seeds
- Salt and black pepper to the taste

Directions:

1. In your slow cooker, mix water with lentils, tomatoes, onion, garlic, turmeric, ginger, cardamom, bay leaf, mustard seeds, onion seeds, fenugreek seeds, fennel seeds, salt and pepper, stir, cover and cook on High for 5 hours.
2. Divide into bowls and serve.

Enjoy!

Nutrition: calories 283, fat 4, fiber 8, carbs 12, protein 4

Rich Jackfruit Dish

Preparation time: 10 minutes
Cooking time: 6 hours
Servings: 4

Ingredients:

- ½ cup tamari
- 40 ounces canned young jackfruit, drained
- ¼ cup coconut aminos
- 1 cup mirin
- ½ cup agave nectar
- 8 garlic cloves, minced
- 2 tablespoons ginger, grated
- 1 yellow onion, chopped
- 4 tablespoons sesame oil
- 1 green pear, cored and chopped
- ½ cup water

Directions:

1. In your slow cooker, mix tamari with jackfruit, aminos, mirin, agave nectar, garlic, ginger, onion, sesame oil, water and pear, stir, cover and cook on Low for 6 hours.
2. Divide into bowls and serve.

Enjoy!

Nutrition: calories 160, fat 4, fiber 1, carbs 20, protein 4

Vegan Gumbo

Preparation time: 10 minutes
Cooking time: 8 hours
Servings: 4

Ingredients:
- 2 tablespoons olive oil
- 1 green bell pepper, chopped
- 1 yellow onion, chopped
- 2 celery stalks, chopped
- 3 garlic cloves, minced
- 15 ounces canned tomatoes, chopped
- 2 cups veggie stock
- 8 ounces white mushrooms, sliced
- 15 ounces canned kidney beans, drained
- 1 zucchini, chopped
- 1 tablespoon Cajun seasoning
- Salt and black pepper to the taste

Directions:
1. In your slow cooker, mix oil with bell pepper, onion, celery, garlic, tomatoes, stock, mushrooms, beans, zucchini, Cajun seasoning, salt and pepper, stir, cover and cook on Low for 8 hours
2. Divide into bowls and serve hot.

Enjoy!

Nutrition: calories 312, fat 4, fiber 7, carbs 19, protein 4

Eggplant Salad

Preparation time: 10 minutes
Cooking time: 8 hours
Servings: 4

Ingredients:
- 24 ounces canned tomatoes, chopped
- 1 red onion, chopped
- 2 red bell peppers, chopped
- 1 big eggplant, roughly chopped
- 1 tablespoon smoked paprika
- 2 teaspoons cumin, ground
- Salt and black pepper to the taste
- Juice of 1 lemon
- 1 tablespoons parsley, chopped

Directions:
1. In your slow cooker, mix tomatoes with onion, bell peppers, eggplant, smoked paprika, cumin, salt, pepper and lemon juice, stir, cover and cook on Low for 8 hours
2. Add parsley, stir, divide into bowls and serve cold as a dinner salad.

Enjoy!

Nutrition: calories 251, fat 4, fiber 6, carbs 8, protein 3

Corn And Cabbage Soup

Preparation time: 10 minutes
Cooking time: 7 hours
Servings: 4

Ingredients:

- 1 small yellow onion, chopped
- 1 tablespoon olive oil
- 2 garlic cloves, minced
- 1 and ½ cups mushrooms, sliced
- 3 teaspoons ginger, grated
- A pinch of salt and black pepper
- 2 cups corn kernels
- 4 cups red cabbage, chopped
- 4 cups water
- 1 tablespoon nutritional yeast
- 2 teaspoons tomato paste
- 1 teaspoon sesame oil
- 1 teaspoon coconut aminos
- 1 teaspoon sriracha sauce

Directions:

1. In your slow cooker, mix olive oil with onion, garlic, mushrooms, ginger, salt, pepper, corn, cabbage, water, yeast and tomato paste, stir, cover and cook on Low for 7 hours.
2. Add sriracha sauce and aminos, stir, leave soup aside for a few minutes, ladle into bowls, drizzle sesame oil all over and serve.

Enjoy!

Nutrition: calories 300, fat 4, fiber 4, carbs 10, protein 4

Okra Soup

Preparation time: 10 minutes
Cooking time: 5 hours
Servings: 6

Ingredients:

- 1 green bell pepper, chopped
- 1 small yellow onion, chopped
- 3 cups veggie stock
- 3 garlic cloves, minced
- 16 ounces okra, sliced
- 2 cup corn
- 29 ounces canned tomatoes, crushed
- 1 and ½ teaspoon smoked paprika
- 1 teaspoon marjoram, dried
- 1 teaspoon thyme, dried
- 1 teaspoon oregano, dried
- Salt and black pepper to the taste

Directions:

1. In your slow cooker, mix bell pepper with onion, stock, garlic, okra, corn, tomatoes, smoked paprika, marjoram, thyme, oregano, salt and pepper, stir, cover and cook on High for 5 hours.
2. Ladle into bowls and serve.

Enjoy!

Nutrition: calories 243, fat 4, fiber 6, carbs 10, protein 3

Carrot Soup

Preparation time: 10 minutes
Cooking time: 5 hours
Servings: 6

Ingredients:

- 2 potatoes, cubed
- 3 pounds carrots, cubed
- 1 yellow onion, chopped
- 1-quart veggie stock
- Salt and black pepper to the taste
- 1 teaspoon thyme, dried
- 3 tablespoons coconut milk
- 2 teaspoons curry powder
- 3 tablespoons vegan cheese, crumbled
- A handful pistachios, chopped

Directions:

1. In your slow cooker, mix onion with potatoes, carrots, stock, salt, pepper, thyme and curry powder, stir, cover, cook on High for 1 hour and on Low for 4 hours.
2. Add coconut milk, stir, blend soup using an immersion blender, ladle soup into bowls, sprinkle vegan cheese and pistachios on top and serve.

Enjoy!

Nutrition: calories 241, fat 4, fiber 7, carbs 10, protein 4

Baby Carrots And Coconut Soup

Preparation time: 10 minutes
Cooking time: 7 hours
Servings: 6

Ingredients:

- 1 sweet potato, cubed
- 2 pounds baby carrots, peeled
- 2 teaspoons ginger paste
- 1 yellow onion, chopped
- 4 cups veggie stock
- 2 teaspoons curry powder
- Salt and black pepper to the taste
- 14 ounces coconut milk

Directions:

1. In your slow cooker, mix sweet potato with baby carrots, ginger paste, onion, stock, curry powder, salt and pepper, stir, cover and cook on High for 7 hours.
2. Add coconut milk, blend soup using an immersion blender, divide soup into bowls and serve.

Enjoy!

Nutrition: calories 100, fat 2, fiber 4, carbs 18, protein 3

Chinese Carrot Cream

Preparation time: 10 minutes
Cooking time: 5 hours
Servings: 6

Ingredients:
- 1 tablespoon coconut oil
- 3 garlic cloves, minced
- 1 yellow onion, chopped
- 1 pound carrots, chopped
- 2 cups veggie stock
- 2 cups water
- Salt and black pepper to the taste
- 1/3 cup peanut butter
- 2 teaspoons chili sauce

Directions:
1. In your slow cooker, mix oil with garlic, onion, carrots, stock, water, salt, pepper and chili sauce, stir, cover and cook on High for 4 hours and 30 minutes.
2. Add peanut butter, stir, cover, cook soup for 30 minutes more, blend using an immersion blender, divide soup into bowls and serve.

Enjoy!

Nutrition: calories 224, fat 14, fiber 6, carbs 18, protein 7

Seitan Stew

Preparation time: 10 minutes
Cooking time: 7 hours
Servings: 4

Ingredients:
- 1 pound seitan, chopped
- 2 tablespoons coconut aminos
- 1 yellow onion, chopped
- 5 cups veggie stock
- 2 tomatoes, chopped
- 3 garlic cloves, minced
- 3 potatoes, cubed
- 3 carrots, chopped
- 2 celery stalks, chopped
- Salt and black pepper to the taste

Directions:
1. In your slow cooker, mix seitan with aminos, onion, stock, tomatoes, garlic, potatoes, carrots, celery, salt and pepper, stir, cover and cook on Low for 7 hours.
2. Divide into bowls and serve.

Enjoy!

Nutrition: calories 300, fat 4, fiber 6, carbs 12, protein 3

Spicy Carrot Stew

Preparation time: 10 minutes
Cooking time: 3 hours
Servings: 6

Ingredients:

- 1 pound carrots, peeled and cut with a spiralizer
- 1 cup red onion, chopped
- 2 garlic cloves, minced
- 2 celery ribs, chopped
- 1 teaspoon coriander, ground
- 1 teaspoon cumin, ground
- ½ teaspoon turmeric, ground
- A pinch of cinnamon powder
- Salt and black pepper to the taste
- 1 cup water
- 4 cups veggie stock
- 1 cup lentils
- 15 ounces canned tomatoes, chopped
- 1 tablespoon tomato paste
- ¼ cup cilantro, chopped
- 1 tablespoon spicy red pepper sauce
- 1 tablespoon lemon juice

Directions:

1. In your slow cooker, mix carrots with onion, garlic, celery, coriander, cumin, turmeric, cinnamon, salt, pepper, water, stock, lentils, tomatoes, tomato paste and pepper sauce, stir, cover and cook on High for 3 hours.
2. Add lemon juice and cilantro, stir, divide into bowls and serve.

Enjoy!

Nutrition: calories 218, fat 4, fiber 4, carbs 8, protein 3

Tomato Soup

Preparation time: 10 minutes
Cooking time: 4 hours
Servings: 6

Ingredients:

- 2 and ¼ pounds tomatoes, chopped
- 3 and ½ cups veggie stock
- 1 yellow onion, chopped
- 2 tablespoons tomato paste
- 2 teaspoons basil, dried
- ½ teaspoon cumin, ground
- Salt and black pepper to the taste
- 2/3 cup almond milk

Directions:

1. In your slow cooker, mix tomatoes with veggie stock, onion, tomato paste, basil, cumin, salt and pepper, stir, cover and cook on Low for 4 hours.
2. Add almond milk, blend soup using an immersion blender, ladle into bowls and serve.

Enjoy!

Nutrition: calories 212, fat 4, fiber 4, carbs 8, protein 5

Classic Tomato Soup

Preparation time: 10 minutes
Cooking time: 8 hours
Servings: 4

Ingredients:

- 1 tablespoon olive oil
- 1 teaspoon garlic, minced
- 1 red bell pepper, chopped
- 1 yellow onion, chopped
- 45 ounces canned tomatoes, chopped
- 1 cup veggie stock
- Salt and black pepper to the taste
- A pinch of red pepper flakes
- 1 tablespoon basil, chopped

Directions:

1. In your slow cooker, mix oil with onion, bell pepper, garlic, tomatoes, stock, salt and pepper, stir, cover and cook on Low for 8 hours.
2. Blend using an immersion blender, add pepper flakes and basil, stir, ladle into bowls and serve.

Enjoy!

Nutrition: calories 100, fat 2, fiber 4, carbs 8, protein 4

Collard Greens Mix

Preparation time: 10 minutes
Cooking time: 3 hours
Servings: 6

Ingredients:

- 1 yellow onion, chopped
- 10 cups collard greens, chopped
- 7 garlic cloves, minced
- 1 cup veggie stock
- 2 tablespoons apple cider vinegar
- 1 tablespoon smoked paprika
- 1 tablespoon chili powder
- A pinch of cayenne pepper
- 1 tablespoon coconut aminos

Directions:

1. In your slow cooker, mix onion with collard greens, garlic, stock, vinegar, paprika, chili powder, cayenne and aminos, stir, cover and cook on Low for 3 hours.
2. Divide between plates and serve.

Enjoy!

Nutrition: calories 172, fat 4, fiber 4, carbs 8, protein 4

Coloured Collard Greens Dish

Preparation time: 10 minutes
Cooking time: 8 hours
Servings: 12

Ingredients:
- 28 ounces veggie stock
- 2 pounds collard greens, chopped
- 2 tablespoons stevia
- ½ cup yellow onion, chopped
- 2 tablespoons apple cider vinegar
- 1 teaspoon red pepper, crushed
- Salt and black pepper to the taste
- 15 ounces canned tomatoes, chopped
- 1 teaspoon smoked paprika
- 1 tablespoon cilantro, chopped

Directions:
1. In your slow cooker, mix collard greens with stock, stevia, onion, vinegar, red pepper, salt, pepper, tomatoes and paprika, stir, cover and cook on Low for 8 hours.
2. Add cilantro, stir, divide on plates and serve.

Enjoy!

Nutrition: calories 200, fat 3, fiber 5, carbs 8, protein 3

Chinese Collard Greens Mix

Preparation time: 10 minutes
Cooking time: 3 hours
Servings: 4

Ingredients:
- 1 cup sweet onion, chopped
- 2 tablespoons olive oil
- 4 garlic cloves, minced
- 4 cups collard greens, chopped
- 1 tablespoon red miso paste
- ¼ cup parsley, chopped
- 1 cup water

Directions:
1. In your slow cooker, mix onion with oil, garlic, collard greens, water and miso paste, stir, cover, cook on High for 1 hour and on Low for 2 hours more.
2. Add parsley, stir, divide between plates and serve.

Enjoy!

Nutrition: calories 200, fat 2, fiber 3, carbs 6, protein 3

Fresh Collard Greens Mix

Preparation time: 10 minutes
Cooking time: 3 hours
Servings: 4

Ingredients:
- 8 cups collard greens, chopped
- 3 tablespoons olive oil
- 1 red onion, chopped
- 2 garlic cloves, minced
- 4 carrots, chopped
- 1 chipotle pepper, chopped
- 1 cup veggie stock
- A pinch of smoked sea salt

Directions:
1. In your slow cooker, mix collard greens with oil, onion, garlic, carrots, chipotle pepper, stock and salt, stir a bit, cover and cook on Low for 3 hours.
2. Divide between plates and serve.

Enjoy!

Nutrition: calories 234, fat 12, fiber 4, carbs 20, protein 5

Artichoke Soup

Preparation time: 10 minutes
Cooking time: 8 hours
Servings: 4

Ingredients:
- 2 celery stalks, chopped
- 1 carrot, chopped
- 1 yellow onion, chopped
- 3 garlic cloves, minced
- ½ teaspoon oregano, dried
- ½ teaspoon rosemary, dried
- ½ teaspoon fennel seeds
- ½ teaspoon thyme, dried
- A pinch of red pepper flakes
- ½ teaspoon garlic powder
- A pinch of salt and black pepper
- 40 ounces canned artichoke hearts, drained and chopped
- 5 and ½ cups veggie stock

Directions:
1. In your slow cooker, mix celery with carrot, onion, garlic, oregano, rosemary, fennel seeds, thyme, pepper flakes, garlic powder, salt, pepper, stock and artichokes, stir, cover and cook on Low for 8 hours.
2. Blend using an immersion blender, ladle into bowls and serve.

Enjoy!

Nutrition: calories 212, fat 3, fiber 5, carbs 6, protein 5

Intense Beet Soup

Preparation time: 10 minutes
Cooking time: 9 hours
Servings: 6

Ingredients:

- 4 beets, chopped
- 28 ounces canned tomatoes, chopped
- 2 potatoes, chopped
- 1 cup baby carrots, chopped
- 3 garlic cloves, minced
- 1 yellow onion, chopped
- Salt and black pepper to the taste
- 1 tablespoon parsley, chopped
- 1 and ½ teaspoons dill, dried
- 1 bay leaf
- 2 tablespoons stevia
- 6 tablespoons red vinegar
- 3 cups green cabbage
- 6 ounces tomato paste

Directions:

1. In your slow cooker, mix beets with tomatoes, potatoes, baby carrots, onion, salt, pepper, dill, bay leaf, stevia, vinegar, tomato paste and green cabbage, stir, cover and cook on Low for 8 hours.
2. Blend soup a bit using an immersion blender, add parsley, stir a bit, ladle into bowls and serve.

Enjoy!

Nutrition: calories 200, fat 3, fiber 6, carbs 5, protein 6

Brussels Sprouts Delight

Preparation time: 10 minutes
Cooking time: 3 hours
Servings: 4

Ingredients:

- 2 pounds Brussels sprouts, halved
- 1 tablespoon almonds, toasted and chopped
- 1 teaspoon red pepper flakes
- ¼ cup coconut aminos
- 2 tablespoons sriracha sauce
- 2 teaspoons garlic powder
- 1 teaspoon onion powder
- 1 tablespoon sweet paprika
- 2 tablespoons sesame oil
- 1 tablespoon balsamic vinegar
- A pinch of salt and black pepper

Directions:

1. In your slow cooker, mix Brussels sprouts with almonds, pepper flakes, aminos, sriracha sauce, garlic powder, onion powder, paprika, oil, vinegar salt and pepper, stir, cover and cook on Low for 3 hours.
2. Divide between plates and serve.

Enjoy!

Nutrition: calories 202, fat 4, fiber 3, carbs 13, protein 3

Mushroom Soup

Preparation time: 10 minutes
Cooking time: 5 hours
Servings: 6

Ingredients:

- 2 yellow onions, chopped
- ¼ cup barley
- 4 cups veggie stock
- 6 ounces brown mushrooms, halved
- A pinch of salt and black pepper
- 3 garlic cloves, minced
- 2 teaspoons thyme, chopped
- 12 ounces cabbage, shredded
- ½ teaspoon smoked paprika
- 4 cups water
- 1 tablespoon lemon juice

Directions:

1. In your slow cooker, mix onion with barley, stock, mushrooms, salt, pepper, garlic, thyme, cabbage, paprika, water and lemon juice, stir, cover and cook on High for 5 hours.
2. Divide soup into bowls and serve.

Enjoy!

Nutrition: calories 200, fat 5, fiber 7, carbs 10, protein 3

Beets And Capers Mix

Preparation time: 10 minutes
Cooking time: 6 hours
Servings: 4

Ingredients:

- 4 beets, peeled and sliced
- 1 cup veggie stock
- 2 tablespoons capers
- 2 tablespoons balsamic vinegar
- A bunch of parsley, chopped
- Salt and black pepper to the taste
- 1 tablespoon olive oil
- 1 garlic clove, chopped

Directions:

1. In your slow cooker, mix beets with stock, vinegar, parsley, capers, salt, pepper, oil and garlic, stir, cover and cook on High for 6 hours.
2. Divide between plates and serve right away.

Enjoy!

Nutrition: calories 101, fat 3, fiber 7, carbs 9, protein 2

Asparagus Soup

Preparation time: 10 minutes
Cooking time: 2 hours
Servings: 4

Ingredients:

- 2 pounds green asparagus, roughly chopped
- 5 veggie stock
- ½ cup coconut milk
- 3 tablespoons olive oil
- Salt and black pepper to the taste
- 1 yellow onion, chopped
- ¼ teaspoon lemon juice

Directions:

1. In your slow cooker, mix asparagus with stock, coconut milk, oil, salt, pepper, onion and lemon juice, stir, cover and cook on High for 2 hours.
2. Divide soup into bowls and serve.

Enjoy!

Nutrition: calories 130, fat 3, fiber 2, carbs 12, protein 3

Fennel Soup

Preparation time: 10 minutes
Cooking time: 4 hours
Servings: 4

Ingredients:

- 2 fennel bulbs, chopped
- 3 cups veggie stock
- 1 teaspoon cumin, ground
- 1 tablespoon olive oil
- Salt and black pepper to the taste
- 2 leeks, chopped

Directions:

1. In your slow cooker, mix fennel with stock, cumin, oil, leeks, salt and pepper, stir, cover and cook on High for 4 hours.
2. Ladle into bowls and serve hot.

Enjoy!

Nutrition: calories 132, fat 2, fiber 5, carbs 11, protein 3

Endives Soup

Preparation time: 10 minutes
Cooking time: 6 hours
Servings: 4

Ingredients:

- 2 tablespoons olive oil
- 2 scallions, chopped
- 3 endives, trimmed and chopped
- 6 cups veggie stock
- 3 garlic cloves chopped
- 1 tablespoon ginger, grated
- 1 teaspoon chili sauce
- A pinch of salt and black pepper
- ½ cup white rice

Directions:

1. In your slow cooker, mix oil with scallions, endives, garlic, stock, ginger, chili sauce, salt, pepper and rice, stir, cover and cook on High for 6 hours.
2. Ladle soup into bowls and serve.

Enjoy!

Nutrition: calories 263., fat 4, fiber 7, carbs 17, protein 3

Vegan Slow Cooker Dessert Recipes

Delicious Cake

Preparation time: 10 minutes
Cooking time: 2 hours and 30 minutes
Servings: 8

Ingredients:

- 1 cup almond flour
- 2 tablespoons cocoa powder
- 1 cup palm sugar
- 2 teaspoons baking powder
- ½ cup chocolate almond milk
- 1 teaspoon vanilla
- 2 tablespoons canola oil
- 1 and ½ cups hot water
- Cooking spray
- ¼ cup cocoa powder

Directions:

1. In a bowl, mix flour with half of the sugar, 2 tablespoons cocoa, baking powder, almond milk, vanilla and canola oil and stir really well.
2. Grease your slow cooker with cooking spray, pour and spread the batter inside.
3. In a bowl, mix the rest of the sugar with hot water and ¼ cup cocoa and stir really well again.
4. Pour this over the batter and also spread.
5. Cover slow cooker and cook on High for 2 hours and 30 minutes.
6. Remove cake from the slow cooker, leave aside to cool down, slice and serve it.

Enjoy!

Nutrition: calories 245, fat 5, fiber 2, carbs 18, protein 3

Strawberry Cobbler

Preparation time: 10 minutes
Cooking time: 2 hours
Servings: 4

Ingredients:

- 2 teaspoons baking powder
- 1 and ¼ cups coconut sugar
- 2 and ½ cups almond flour
- ½ teaspoon cinnamon powder
- 2 tablespoons flax seed meal mixed with 1 tablespoon water
- ½ cup almond milk
- 4 tablespoons canola oil
- 6 cups strawberries, chopped
- ¼ cup rolled oats
- ¼ cup basil, chopped
- Cooking spray

Directions:

1. In a bowl, mix 2 cups flour with ¼ cup sugar, baking powder, cinnamon, milk, oil and flax seed meal and stir really well.
2. In another bowl, mix the rest of the flour with the rest of the sugar, basil and strawberries and toss well.
3. Pour the batter into your slow cooker after you've sprayed with cooking spray and spread well.
4. Add strawberries mix on top, sprinkle rolled oats, cover and cook on High for 2 hours.
5. Leave cobbler to cool down a bit and serve.

Nutrition: calories 130, fat 4, fiber 3, carbs 8, protein 7

Spicy Pears

Preparation time: 10 minutes
Cooking time: 4 hours
Servings: 2

Ingredients:

- 2 cups orange juice
- 4 pears, peeled and cored
- 5 cardamom pods
- ¼ cup maple syrup
- 1 cinnamon stick
- 1 small ginger piece, grated

Directions:

1. Place pears in your slow cooker.
2. Add cardamom, orange juice, maple syrup, cinnamon and ginger, cover and cook on Low for 4 hours.
3. Divide pears between plates and serve.

Enjoy!

Nutrition: calories 130, fat 2, fiber 3, carbs 6, protein 4

Delicious Apples

Preparation time: 10 minutes
Cooking time: 2 hours
Servings: 5

Ingredients:

- 5 apples, cored
- 2 tablespoons coconut butter, melted
- 5 cups vegan granola
- 5 teaspoons maple syrup

Directions:

1. Place apples in your slow cooker and drizzle the melted coconut butter all over them.
2. Stuff them with granola and drizzle the maple syrup at the end.
3. Cover and cook on High for 2 hours.
4. Divide apples on plates and serve.

Enjoy!

Nutrition: calories 200, fat 3, fiber 3, carbs 7, protein 8

Fruit Compote

Preparation time: 10 minutes
Cooking time: 4 hours
Servings: 6

Ingredients:

- 1-quart water
- 1 cup coconut sugar
- 1 pound mixed apples, pears and cranberries, dried
- 5-star anise
- 2 cinnamon sticks
- Zest from 1 orange, grated
- A pinch cloves, ground
- Zest from 1 lemon, grated

Directions:

1. Put the water and the sugar in your slow cooker and stir well.
2. Add dried fruits, star anise, cinnamon, orange and lemon zest and cloves.
3. Stir, cover and cook on High for 4 hours.
4. Serve your compote warm in small dessert cups.

Enjoy!

Nutrition: calories 110, fat 0, fiber 2, carbs 3, protein 5

Pumpkin Pudding

Preparation time: 10 minutes
Cooking time: 4 hours
Servings: 6

Ingredients:

- 8 cups vegan bread cubes
- ½ cup cinnamon chips
- Cooking spray
- ½ cup pecans, toasted and chopped
- 2 tablespoons flaxseed meal mixed with 1 tablespoon water
- 1 cup canned pumpkin flesh, chopped
- 1 cup coconut milk
- ½ cup palm sugar
- ½ cup coconut butter
- 1 teaspoon vanilla extract
- ½ teaspoon cinnamon powder
- ¼ teaspoon ginger powder
- ½ teaspoon nutmeg, ground
- A pinch of cloves, ground

Directions:

1. Grease your slow cooker with cooking spray and spread bread cubes on the bottom.
2. Add cinnamon chips and pecans, stir a bit and leave aside for now.
3. Meanwhile, in a bowl, mix flax seed meal with pumpkin, coconut cream, palm sugar, coconut butter, vanilla extract, cinnamon powder, ginger, nutmeg and cloves and stir well.
4. Spread these over bread cubes in the slow cooker, cover and cook on Low for 4 hours.
5. Divide pudding into bowls when it cools down a bit and serve.

Enjoy!

Nutrition: calories 200, fat 3, fiber 3, carbs 6, protein 9

Delicious Peanut Butter Cake

Preparation time: 10 minutes
Cooking time: 2 hours and 30 minutes
Servings: 6

Ingredients:

- 1 cup almond flour
- ½ cup coconut sugar
- ¾ cup coconut sugar
- 3 tablespoons cocoa powder
- ¼ cup cocoa powder
- 1 and ½ teaspoons baking powder
- 2 tablespoons vegan margarine, melted
- ½ cup soy milk
- 1 teaspoon vanilla extract
- ½ cup peanut butter
- 2 cups hot water
- Cooking spray

Directions:

1. In a bowl, mix flour with ½ cup sugar, baking powder and 3 tablespoons cocoa powder and stir well.
2. Add margarine, soy milk and vanilla and stir well.
3. Grease your slow cooker with cooking spray and pour the cake mix in it.
4. In another bowl, mix ¼ cup cocoa powder with ¾ cup sugar and stir.
5. In a second bowl, mix peanut butter with hot water and whisk really well.
6. Combine cocoa powder mix with peanut butter one and stir everything.
7. Pour this over your cake batter, cover and cook on High for 2 hours and 30 minutes.
8. Leave the cake to cool down a bit, slice and serve.

Enjoy!

Nutrition: calories 220, fat 3, fiber 4, carbs 6, protein 10

Tasty Apple Crisp

Preparation time: 10 minutes
Cooking time: 3 hours
Servings: 6

Ingredients:

- 6 apples, cored, peeled and sliced
- 1 and ½ cups almond flour
- Cooking spray
- 1 cup palm sugar
- ½ teaspoon nutmeg, ground
- 1 tablespoon cinnamon powder
- ¼ teaspoon ginger powder
- ¾ cup coconut butter, melted

Directions:

1. Grease your slow cooker with cooking spray and arrange apple slices on it.
2. In a bowl, mix flour with palm sugar, ginger, cinnamon, nutmeg and coconut butter and stir using your hands.
3. Spread this mix over your apple slices, cover slow cooker and cook on High for 3 hours.
4. Divide into dessert bowls and serve.

Enjoy!

Nutrition: calories 160, fat 5, fiber 5, carbs 12, protein 6

Delicious Peach Cake

Preparation time: 10 minutes
Cooking time: 2 hours and 30 minutes
Servings: 8

Ingredients:

- 10 tablespoons coconut butter, melted
- 45 ounces canned peaches, drained
- 1 and 2/3 cup palm sugar
- 1 teaspoon cinnamon powder
- ½ teaspoon nutmeg
- ½ teaspoon almond extract
- 2 teaspoons baking powder
- 2 tablespoons flaxseed meal mixed with 1 tablespoon water
- 2 cups almond flour
- 1 cup coconut milk

Directions:

1. Drizzle half of the butter on the bottom of your slow cooker.
2. In a bowl mix nutmeg with 2/3 cup sugar and cinnamon and stir well.
3. Spread this over the butter in your slow cooker.
4. Arrange peaches next and spread them evenly in the pot.
5. In a bowl, mix the rest of the butter with the rest of the sugar, coconut milk, almond extract and flaxseed meal and stir well.
6. In another bowl, mix flour with baking powder and stir.
7. Combine butter and sugar mix with the flour and stir well.
8. Pour this over the peaches, cover and cook on High for 2 hours and 30 minutes.
9. Leave the cake to cool down a bit and turn it upside down on a platter.
10. Serve cold.

Nutrition: calories 200, fat 4, fiber 5, carbs 7, protein 8

Delicious Blueberry Pudding

Preparation time: 10 minutes
Cooking time: 3 hours
Servings: 6

Ingredients:

- 1 cup almond flour
- 2 tablespoons lemon juice
- 2 cups blueberries
- 2 teaspoons baking powder
- ½ teaspoon nutmeg, ground
- ½ cup almond milk
- 1 and ¾ cup coconut sugar
- 1 tablespoon flax seed meal mixed with 1 tablespoon water
- ¼ cup coconut butter, melted
- 1 teaspoon vanilla extract
- 1 tablespoon vegan cornstarch
- 1 cup hot water
- Cooking spray

Directions:

1. Grease your slow cooker with cooking spray, add blueberries and lemon juice, toss a bit and spread them evenly on the bottom of the pot.
2. In a bowl, mix flour with nutmeg, ¾ cup sugar and baking powder and stir.
3. Add vanilla, coconut butter, flaxseed meal and milk and stir well again.
4. Pour this over blueberries and spread.
5. In a small bowl, mix the rest of the sugar with cornstarch and hot water and stir really well.
6. Pour this into your slow cooker as well, cover and cook on High for 3 hours.
7. Leave pudding to cool down a bit, divide into bowls and serve

Nutrition: calories 220, fat 4, fiber 4, carbs 9, protein 6

Tasty Pear Delight

Preparation time: 10 minutes
Cooking time: 4 hours
Servings: 12

Ingredients:

- 3 pears, cored, peeled and chopped
- ½ cup raisins
- 2 cups dried fruits, mixed
- ¼ cup coconut sugar
- 1 tablespoon vinegar
- 1 teaspoon lemon zest, grated
- 1 teaspoon ginger powder
- A pinch of cinnamon powder

Directions:

1. Put the pears in your slow cooker.
2. Add raisins, fruits, sugar, vinegar, lemon zest, ginger powder and cinnamon, stir, cover and cook on Low for 4 hours.
3. Divide into small jars and serve whenever!

Enjoy!

Nutrition: calories 140, fat 3, fiber 4, carbs 6, protein 6

Easy Almond Pudding

Preparation time: 10 minutes
Cooking time: 2 hours and 30 minutes
Servings: 6

Ingredients:

- 1 mandarin, sliced
- Juice from 2 mandarins
- 2 tablespoons coconut sugar
- 4 ounces coconut butter, soft
- 2 tablespoons flax seed meal mixed with 1 tablespoon water
- ¾ cup coconut sugar
- ¾ cup almond flour
- 1 teaspoon baking powder
- ¾ cup almonds, ground
- Cooking spray

Directions:

1. Grease a loaf pan cooking spray and sprinkle 2 tablespoons sugar on the bottom.
2. Arrange sliced Mandarin over the sugar and leave loaf pan aside for now.
3. In a bowl, mix butter with ¾ cup sugar and flax seed meal mixed with water and stir really well.
4. Add almonds, flour, baking powder and the mandarin juice and stir again.
5. Spread this over mandarin slices, arrange pan in your slow cooker, cover and cook on High for 2 hours and 30 minutes.
6. Uncover, leave aside for a few minutes, transfer to a platter, slice and serve.

Enjoy!

Nutrition: calories 200, fat 4, fiber 2, carbs 5, protein 6

Delicious Cinnamon Casserole

Preparation time: 10 minutes
Cooking time: 3 hours
Servings: 8

Ingredients:

- 1 teaspoon cinnamon powder
- 12 ounces vegan cinnamon roll dough, cut in quarters
- 2 tablespoons flax seed meal mixed with 1 tablespoon water
- ½ cup coconut cream
- Cooking spray
- 3 tablespoons maple syrup
- ½ teaspoon nutmeg
- 2 teaspoons vanilla extract
- 1/3 cup pecans, chopped

Directions:

1. Grease your slow cooker with cooking spray and add cinnamon roll pieces.
2. In a bowl, mix flax seed meal with coconut cream, vanilla, nutmeg, maple syrup and cinnamon and stir.
3. Spread this over cinnamon rolls, sprinkle pecans on top, cover and cook on Low for 3 hours.
4. Divide between plates and serve cinnamon rolls warm.

Enjoy!

Nutrition: calories 200, fat 3, fiber 4, carbs 6, protein 9

Strawberry Jam

Preparation time: 10 minutes
Cooking time: 3 hours
Servings: 12

Ingredients:

- 2 tablespoons lemon juice
- 4 pints strawberries
- 4 cups coconut sugar

Directions:

1. Put strawberries in your slow cooker.
2. Add lemon juice and stir gently.
3. Add sugar, stir again, cover and cook on Low for 1 hour.
4. Stir and cook on Low for 1 more hour.
5. Stir again and cook for 1 last hour.
6. Divide into jars and serve whenever you like.

Enjoy!

Nutrition: calories 30, fat 0, fiber 1, carbs 6, protein 1

Amazing Hot Fruits

Preparation time: 10 minutes
Cooking time: 4 hours
Servings: 10

Ingredients:

- 20 ounces canned pineapple chunks, drained
- 21 ounces canned cherries, drained
- 15 ounces canned apricots, halved and drained
- 15 ounces canned peach slices, drained
- 25 ounces vegan applesauce
- 15 ounces canned mandarin oranges, drained
- ¼ cup coconut sugar
- 1 teaspoon cinnamon powder

Directions:

1. Put pineapple pieces in your slow cooker.
2. Add cherries, apricots, peaches, applesauce, oranges, cinnamon and sugar.
3. Stir gently, cover and cook on Low for 4 hours.
4. Divide into bowls and serve warm.

Enjoy!

Nutrition: calories 200, fat 3, fiber 2, carbs 10, protein 2

Stewed Plums

Preparation time: 10 minutes
Cooking time: 3 hours
Servings: 6

Ingredients:

- 14 plums, halved and pitted
- 1 and ¼ cups coconut sugar
- 1 teaspoon cinnamon, ground
- ¼ cup water
- 2 tablespoons vegan cornstarch

Directions:

1. Put plums in your slow cooker.
2. Add sugar, cinnamon, water and cornstarch, stir, cover and cook on Low for 3 hours.
3. Divide into small jars, seal them and serve as a dessert.

Enjoy!

Nutrition: calories 100, fat 2, fiber 1, carbs 4, protein 8

Plums and Apples Surprise

Preparation time: 10 minutes
Cooking time: 3 hours
Servings: 4

Ingredients:

- 1 and ½ pounds plums, pitted and halved
- ½ cup agave nectar
- 2 apples, cored, peeled and cut into wedges
- 1 cinnamon stick
- 2 tablespoons lemon zest, grated
- 2 teaspoons balsamic vinegar
- 1 cup hot water

Directions:

1. In your slow cooker, mix plums with apples, agave nectar, cinnamon stick, lemon zest, water and balsamic vinegar.
2. Stir, cover and cook on Low for 3 hours.
3. Discard cinnamon stick, divide this into small dessert bowls and serve with some vegan yogurt on top.

Enjoy!

Nutrition: calories 100, fat 1, fiber 2, carbs 5, protein 2

Wonderful Plum Butter

Preparation time: 10 minutes
Cooking time: 10 hours
Servings: 10

Ingredients:

- 4 pounds plums, pitted and halved
- 1 cup water
- 1 teaspoon cinnamon, ground
- ½ teaspoon cardamom, ground
- 1 cup palm sugar

Directions:

1. Put plums and water in your slow cooker.
2. Cover and cook on Low for 1 hour.
3. Stir, add cinnamon, sugar and cardamom, stir, cover and cook on Low for 9 more hours.
4. Stir really well, divide into jars and serve.

Enjoy!

Nutrition: calories 100, fat 2, fiber 1, carbs 3, protein 6

Delicious Banana Dessert

Preparation time: 10 minutes
Cooking time: 2 hours
Servings: 4

Ingredients:

- Juice of ½ lemon
- 3 tablespoons agave nectar
- 1 tablespoon coconut oil
- 4 bananas, peeled and sliced diagonally
- ½ teaspoon cardamom seeds
- Chopped almonds for serving

Directions:

1. Put bananas in your slow cooker.
2. Add agave nectar, lemon juice, oil and cardamom.
3. Stir gently, cover and cook on Low for 2 hours.
4. Divide into bowls and serve with chopped almonds on top.

Enjoy!

Nutrition: calories 100, fat 1, fiber 2, carbs 10, protein 1

Stewed Rhubarb

Preparation time: 10 minutes
Cooking time: 7 hours
Servings: 4

Ingredients:

- 5 cups rhubarb, chopped
- 2 tablespoons coconut butter
- 1/3 cup water
- 2/3 cup coconut sugar
- 1 teaspoon vanilla extract

Directions:

1. Put rhubarb in your slow cooker.
2. Add water and sugar, stir gently, cover and cook on Low for 7 hours.
3. Add coconut butter and vanilla extract, stir and keep in the fridge until it's cold.

Enjoy!

Nutrition: calories 120, fat 2, fiber 3, carbs 6, protein 1

Pudding Cake

Preparation time: 10 minutes
Cooking time: 2 hours and 30 minutes
Servings: 8

Ingredients:
- 1 and ½ cup stevia
- 1 cup flour
- ¼ cup baking cocoa+ 2 tablespoons
- ½ cup chocolate almond milk
- 2 teaspoons baking powder
- 2 tablespoons canola oil
- 1 teaspoon vanilla extract
- 1 and ½ cups hot water
- Cooking spray

Directions:
1. In a bowl, mix flour with 2 tablespoons cocoa, baking powder, almond milk, oil and vanilla extract, whisk well and spread on the bottom of the slow cooker after you've greased with cooking spray.
2. In a separate bowl, mix stevia with the rest of the cocoa and the water, whisk well and spread over the batter in your slow cooker.
3. Cover, cook your cake on High for 2 hours and 30 minutes.
4. Leave cake to cool down, slice and serve.

Enjoy!

Nutrition: calories 250, fat 4, fiber 3, carbs 40, protein 2

Sweet Peanut Butter Cake

Preparation time: 10 minutes
Cooking time: 2 hours and 30 minutes
Servings: 8

Ingredients:
- 1 cup coconut sugar
- 1 cup flour
- 3 tablespoons cocoa powder+ ½ cup
- 1 and ½ teaspoons baking powder
- ½ cup almond milk
- 2 tablespoons coconut oil
- 2 cups hot water
- 1 teaspoon vanilla extract
- ½ cup peanut butter
- Cooking spray

Directions:
1. In a bowl, mix half of the coconut sugar with 3 tablespoons cocoa, flour and baking powder and stir well.
2. Add coconut oil, vanilla and milk, stir well and pour into your slow cooker greased with cooking spray.
3. In another bowl, mix the rest of the sugar with the rest of the cocoa, peanut butter and hot water, stir well and pour over the batter in the slow cooker.
4. Cover pot, cook on High for 2 hours and 30 minutes, slice cake and serve.

Enjoy!

Nutrition: calories 242, fat 4, fiber 7, carbs 8, protein 4

Blueberry Cake

Preparation time: 10 minutes
Cooking time: 1 hour
Servings: 6

Ingredients:

- ½ cup whole wheat flour
- ¼ teaspoon baking powder
- ¼ teaspoon stevia
- ¼ cup blueberries
- 1/3 cup almond milk
- 1 teaspoon olive oil
- 1 teaspoon flaxseed, ground
- ½ teaspoon lemon zest, grated
- ¼ teaspoon vanilla extract
- ¼ teaspoon lemon extract
- Cooking spray

Directions:

1. In a bowl, mix flour with baking powder and stevia and stir.
2. Add blueberries, milk, oil, flaxseeds, lemon zest, vanilla extract and lemon extract and whisk well.
3. Spray your slow cooker with cooking spray, line it with parchment paper, pour cake batter, cover pot and cook on High for 1 hour.
4. Leave cake to cool down, slice and serve.

Enjoy!

Nutrition: calories 200, fat 4, fiber 4, carbs 10, protein 4

Peach Cobbler

Preparation time: 10 minutes
Cooking time: 4 hours
Servings: 4

Ingredients:

- 4 cups peaches, peeled and sliced
- ¼ cup coconut sugar
- ½ teaspoon cinnamon powder
- 1 and ½ cups vegan sweet crackers, crushed
- ¼ cup stevia
- ¼ teaspoon nutmeg, ground
- ½ cup almond milk
- 1 teaspoon vanilla extract
- Cooking spray

Directions:

1. In a bowl, mix peaches with coconut sugar and cinnamon and stir.
2. In a separate bowl, mix crackers with stevia, nutmeg, almond milk and vanilla extract and stir.
3. Spray your slow cooker with cooking spray and spread peaches on the bottom.
4. Add crackers mix, spread, cover and cook on Low for 4 hours.
5. Divide cobbler between plates and serve.

Enjoy!

Nutrition: calories 212, fat 4, fiber 4, carbs 7, protein 3

Apple Mix

Preparation time: 10 minutes
Cooking time: 4 hours
Servings: 6

Ingredients:
- 6 apples, cored, peeled and sliced
- 1 and ½ cups almond flour
- Cooking spray
- 1 cup coconut sugar
- 1 tablespoon cinnamon powder
- ¾ cup cashew butter, melted

Directions:
1. Add apple slices to your slow cooker after you've greased it with cooking spray
2. Add flour, sugar, cinnamon and coconut butter, stir gently, cover, cook on High for 4 hours, divide into bowls and serve cold.

Enjoy!

Nutrition: calories 200, fat 5, fiber 5, carbs 8, protein 4

Pears and Dried Fruits Bowls

Preparation time: 10 minutes
Cooking time: 4 hours
Servings: 12

Ingredients:
- 3 pears, cored and chopped
- ½ cup raisins
- 2 cups dried fruits
- 1 teaspoon ginger powder
- ¼ cup coconut sugar
- 1 teaspoon lemon zest, grated

Directions:
1. In your slow cooker, mix pears with raisins, dried fruits, ginger, sugar and lemon zest, stir, cover, cook on Low for 4 hours, divide into bowls and serve cold.

Enjoy!

Nutrition: calories 140, fat 3, fiber 4, carbs 6, protein 6

Strawberry Stew

Preparation time: 10 minutes
Cooking time: 3 hours
Servings: 10

Ingredients:

- 2 tablespoons lemon juice
- 2 pounds strawberries
- 4 cups coconut sugar

- 1 teaspoon cinnamon powder
- 1 teaspoon vanilla extract

Directions:

1. In your slow cooker, mix strawberries with coconut sugar, lemon juice, cinnamon and vanilla, stir gently, cover and cook on Low for 3 hours.
2. Divide into bowls and serve cold.

Enjoy!

Nutrition: calories 100, fat 0, fiber 1, carbs 2, protein 2

Poached Plums

Preparation time: 10 minutes
Cooking time: 3 hours
Servings: 6

Ingredients:

- 14 plums, halved
- 1 and ¼ cups coconut sugar

- 1 teaspoon cinnamon powder
- ¼ cup water

Directions:

1. Arrange plums in your slow cooker, add sugar, cinnamon and water, stir, cover, cook on Low for 3 hours, divide into cups and serve cold.

Enjoy!

Nutrition: calories 150, fat 2, fiber 1, carbs 2, protein 3

Bananas And Agave Sauce

Preparation time: 10 minutes
Cooking time: 2 hours
Servings: 4

Ingredients:

- Juice of ½ lemon
- 3 tablespoons agave nectar
- 1 tablespoon coconut oil
- 4 bananas, peeled and sliced diagonally
- ½ teaspoon cardamom seeds

Directions:

1. Arrange bananas in your slow cooker, add agave nectar, lemon juice, oil and cardamom, cover and cook on Low for 2 hours.
2. Divide bananas on plates, drizzle agave sauce all over and serve.

Enjoy!

Nutrition: calories 120, fat 1, fiber 2, carbs 8, protein 3

Orange Cake

Preparation time: 10 minutes
Cooking time: 5 hours
Servings: 4

Ingredients:

- Cooking spray
- 1 teaspoon baking powder
- 1 cup almond flour
- 1 cup coconut sugar
- ½ teaspoon cinnamon powder
- 3 tablespoons coconut oil, melted
- ½ cup almond milk
- ½ cup pecans, chopped
- ¾ cup water
- ½ cup raisins
- ½ cup orange peel, grated
- ¾ cup orange juice

Directions:

1. In a bowl, mix flour with half of the sugar, baking powder, cinnamon, 2 tablespoons oil, milk, pecans and raisins, stir and pour this in your slow cooker after you've sprayed it with cooking spray.
2. Heat up a small pan over medium heat, add water, orange juice, orange peel, the rest of the oil and the rest of the sugar, stir, bring to a boil, pour over the mix in the slow cooker, cover and cook on Low for 5 hours.
3. Divide into dessert bowls and serve cold.

Enjoy!

Nutrition: calories 182, fat 3, fiber 1, carbs 4, protein 3

Stewed Apples

Preparation time: 10 minutes
Cooking time: 1 hour and 30 minutes
Servings: 5

Ingredients:

- 5 apples, tops cut off and cored
- 5 figs
- 1/3 cup coconut sugar
- ¼ cup pecans, chopped
- 2 teaspoons lemon zest, grated
- ½ teaspoon cinnamon powder
- 1 tablespoon lemon juice
- 1tablespoon coconut oil
- ½ cup water

Directions:

1. Arrange apples in your slow cooker.
2. Add figs, coconut sugar, pecans, lemon zest, cinnamon, lemon juice, coconut oil and water, toss, cover and cook on High for 1 hour and 30 minutes.
3. Divide apples and sauce on plates and serve.

Enjoy!

Nutrition: calories 170, fat 1, fiber 2, carbs 6, protein 3

Pears And Orange Sauce

Preparation time: 10 minutes
Cooking time: 4 hours
Servings: 4

Ingredients:

- 4 pears, peeled and cored
- 2 cups orange juice
- ¼ cup maple syrup
- 2 teaspoons cinnamon powder
- 1 tablespoon ginger, grated

Directions:

1. In your slow cooker, mix pears with orange juice, maple syrup, cinnamon and ginger, cover and cook on Low for 4 hours.
2. Divide pears and orange sauce between plates and serve warm.

Enjoy!

Nutrition: calories 140, fat 1, fiber 2, carbs 3, protein 4

Almond Cookies

Preparation time: 10 minutes
Cooking time: 2 hours and 30 minutes
Servings: 12

Ingredients:

- 1 tablespoon flaxseed mixed with 2 tablespoons water
- ¼ cup coconut oil, melted
- 1 cup coconut sugar
- ½ teaspoon vanilla extract
- 1 teaspoon baking powder
- 1 and ½ cups almond meal
- ½ cup almonds, chopped

Directions:

1. In a bowl, mix oil with sugar, vanilla extract and flax meal and whisk.
2. Add baking powder, almond meal and almonds and stir well.
3. Line your slow cooker with parchment paper, spread cookie mix on the bottom of the pot, cover and cook on Low for 2 hours and 30 minutes.
4. Leave cookie sheet to cool down, cut into medium pieces and serve.

Enjoy!

Nutrition: calories 220, fat 2, fiber 1, carbs 3, protein 6

Pumpkin Cake

Preparation time: 10 minutes
Cooking time: 2 hours and 20 minutes
Servings: 10

Ingredients:

- 1 and ½ teaspoons baking powder
- Cooking spray
- 1 cup pumpkin puree
- 2 cups almond flour
- ½ teaspoon baking soda
- 1 and ½ teaspoons cinnamon, ground
- ¼ teaspoon ginger, ground
- 1 tablespoon coconut oil, melted
- 1 tablespoon flaxseed mixed with 2 tablespoons water
- 1 tablespoon vanilla extract
- 1/3 cup maple syrup
- 1 teaspoon lemon juice

Directions:

1. In a bowl, flour with baking powder, baking soda, cinnamon and ginger and stir.
2. Add flaxseed, coconut oil, vanilla, pumpkin puree, maple syrup and lemon juice, stir and pour in your slow cooker after you've sprayed it with cooking spray and lined with parchment paper.
3. Cover pot and cook on Low for 2 hours and 20 minutes.
4. Leave cake to cool down, slice and serve.

Enjoy!

Nutrition: calories 182, fat 3, fiber 2, carbs 3, protein 1

Strawberries Jam

Preparation time: 10 minutes
Cooking time: 4 hours
Servings: 10

Ingredients:
- 32 ounces strawberries, chopped
- 2 pounds coconut sugar
- Zest of 1 lemon, grated
- 4 ounces raisins
- 3 ounces water

Directions:
1. In your slow cooker, mix strawberries with coconut sugar, lemon zest, raisins and water, stir, cover and cook on High for 4 hours.
2. Divide into small jars and serve cold.

Enjoy!

Nutrition: calories 100, fat 3, fiber 2, carbs 2, protein 1

Lemon Jam

Preparation time: 10 minutes
Cooking time: 3 hours
Servings: 10

Ingredients:
- 2 pounds lemons, washed, peeled and sliced
- 2 pounds coconut sugar
- 1 tablespoon vinegar

Directions:
1. In your slow cooker, mix lemons with coconut sugar and vinegar, stir, cover and cook on High for 3 hours.
2. Divide into jars and serve cold.

Enjoy!

Nutrition: calories 100, fat 0, fiber 2, carbs 7, protein 4

Strawberries And Rhubarb Marmalade

Preparation time: 10 minutes
Cooking time: 3 hours
Servings: 8

Ingredients:
- 1/3 cup water
- 2 pounds rhubarb, chopped
- 2 pounds strawberries, chopped
- 1 cup coconut sugar
- 1 tablespoon mint, chopped

Directions:
1. In your slow cooker, mix water with rhubarb, strawberries, sugar and mint, stir, cover and cook on High for 3 hours.
2. Divide into cups and serve cold.

Enjoy!

Nutrition: calories 100, fat 1, fiber 4, carbs 10, protein 2

Sweet Potatoes Pudding

Preparation time: 10 minutes
Cooking time: 5 hours
Servings: 8

Ingredients:
- 1 cup water
- 1 tablespoon lemon peel, grated
- ½ cup coconut sugar
- 3 sweet potatoes peeled and sliced
- ¼ cup cashew butter
- ¼ cup maple syrup
- 1 cup pecans, chopped

Directions:
1. In your slow cooker, mix water with lemon peel, coconut sugar, potatoes, cashew butter, maple syrup and pecans, stir, cover and cook on High for 5 hours.
2. Divide sweet potato pudding into bowls and serve cold.

Enjoy!

Nutrition: calories 200, fat 4, fiber 3, carbs 10, protein 4

Cherry Marmalade

Preparation time: 10 minutes
Cooking time: 3 hours
Servings: 6

Ingredients:
- 2 tablespoons lemon juice
- 3 tablespoons vegan gelatin
- 4 cups cherries, pitted
- 2 cups coconut sugar

Directions:
1. In your slow cooker, mix lemon juice with gelatin, cherries and coconut sugar, stir, cover and cook on High for 3 hours.
2. Divide into cups and serve cold.

Enjoy!

Nutrition: calories 211, fat 3, fiber 1, carbs 3, protein 3

Rice Pudding

Preparation time: 10 minutes
Cooking time: 5 hours
Servings: 4

Ingredients:
- 6 and ½ cups water
- 1 cup coconut sugar
- 2 cups white rice, washed and rinsed
- 2 cinnamon sticks
- ½ cup coconut, shredded

Directions:
1. In your slow cooker, mix water with coconut sugar, rice, cinnamon and coconut, stir, cover and cook on High for 5 hours.
2. Divide pudding into cups and serve cold.

Enjoy!

Nutrition: calories 213, fat 4, fiber 6, carbs 9, protein 4

Conclusion

Veganism can be such a fun diet and it can become your lifestyle in no time!
It might sound difficult at the beginning but you will soon get used to not eating meat and anything related to it.
Veganism will become a part of your life and you will learn to embrace it.

On the other hand, slow cooking is a modern cooking method that allows you to prepare the best dishes in the world.
Slow cooking has gained a lot of popularity over the last years due to the fact that it helps you cook healthy and fresh dishes.

Now, the question you need to ask yourself is: what do you get from combining a veganism and slow cooking?
Don't you know by now? You get the best cookbook ever!
So, go and get your own copy today and start your new and improved vegan life!

Recipe Index

3

3 Bean Chili, 96

A

Acorn Squash And Great Sauce, 47

Almond and Beans Fondue, 51

Almond Butter Oatmeal, 29

Almond Cookies, 131

Amazing Carrots Surprise, 35

Amazing Curry, 78

Amazing Hot Fruits, 122

Amazing Mushroom Stew, 68

Amazing Potato Dish, 65

Appetizer Potato Salad, 60

Apple Crumble, 13

Apple Granola, 31

Apple Mix, 127

Artichoke Soup, 110

Artichoke Spread, 62

Asparagus Soup, 113

Autumn Veggie Mix, 79

B

Baby Carrots And Coconut Soup, 105

Banana Oatmeal, 30

Bananas And Agave Sauce, 129

Beans in Rich Tomato Sauce, 51

Beans, Carrots and Spinach Side Dish, 39

Beets And Capers Mix, 112

Beets And Carrots, 46

Black Bean Appetizer Salad, 61

Black Beans, Rice And Mango, 86

Black Eyed Peas Pate, 57

Black Eyed Peas Stew, 71

Blueberries Oatmeal, 28

Blueberry Cake, 126

Breakfast Cherry Delight, 8

Breakfast Chia Pudding, 33

Breakfast Enchiladas, 22

Breakfast Energy Bars, 15

Breakfast Fajitas, 21

Breakfast Quinoa Pudding, 19

Breakfast Tofu Casserole, 27

Brown Rice Soup, 97

Brussels Sprouts, 45

Brussels Sprouts Delight, 111

Bulgur Chili, 94

Butternut Squash Soup, 98

Butternut Squash Spread, 54

C

Candied Almonds, 50

Caribbean Dish, 89

Carrot And Zucchini Oatmeal, 31

Carrot and Zucchini Surprising Breakfast, 14

Carrot Oatmeal, 27

Carrot Soup, 105

Cashew And White Bean Spread, 54

Cauliflower And Broccoli Side Dish, 40

Cauliflower Chili, 95

Chard And Sweet Potato Soup, 99

Cherry Marmalade, 134

Chickpeas And Veggies, 43

Chickpeas Delight, 90

Chickpeas Soup, 73

Chinese Carrot Cream, 106

Chinese Collard Greens Mix, 109

Chinese Soup And Ginger Sauce, 100

Chinese Tofu and Veggies, 70

Chipotle Tacos, 49

Chowder, 59

Classic Black Beans Chili, 64

Classic Tomato Soup, 108

Collard Greens Delight, 34

Collard Greens Mix, 108

Colored Collard Greens Dish, 109

Colored Stuffed Bell Peppers, 61

Corn And Cabbage Soup, 104

Corn Cream Soup, 100

Corn Dip, 62

Cornbread Casserole, 17

Cranberry Breakfast Quinoa, 32

Cranberry French Toast, 25

Crazy Cauliflower and Zucchini Surprise, 76

Crazy Maple and Pear Breakfast, 9

Creamy Corn, 48

D

Delicious Apples, 116

Delicious Baked Beans, 67

Delicious Banana and Coconut Milk Delight, 13

Delicious Banana Bread, 15

Delicious Banana Dessert, 124

Delicious Barley and Squash Gratin, 38

Delicious Blueberry Pudding, 119

Delicious Breakfast Quinoa, 12

Delicious Butternut Squash Soup, 68

Delicious Cake, 115

Delicious Chard Soup, 70

Delicious Cinnamon Casserole, 121

Delicious Coconut Porridge, 22

Delicious Corn Dip, 53

Delicious Eggplant Salad, 74

Delicious Mashed Potatoes, 38

Delicious Oat Meal, 8

Delicious Peach Cake, 119

Delicious Peanut Butter Cake, 118

Delicious Pear Oatmeal, 24

Delicious Pumpkin Butter, 12

Delicious Quinoa And Oats, 32

Delicious Tapioca Pudding, 17

Delicious Vegan Frittata, 30

Delicious Vegan Scramble, 28

Divine Carrot Oatmeal, 11

E

Easy Almond Pudding, 120

Easy Lentils Mix, 82

Easy Sweet Potatoes Dish, 37

Eggplant And Kale Mix, 44

Eggplant Appetizer, 55

Eggplant Salad, 103

Eggplant Tapenade, 50

Endives Soup, 114

F

Fennel Soup, 113

Flavored Beets, 36

Fresh Collard Greens Mix, 110

Fruit Compote, 117

G

Glazed Carrots, 42

Great Beans and Lentils Dish, 36

Great Bolognese Dip, 56

Green Beans Soup, 98

Green Chili Soup, 89

H

Healthy Steel Cut Oats, 26

Hearty Breakfast Casserole, 23

Hearty French Toast Bowls, 9

Hot and Delicious Soup, 74

Hummus, 58

I

Incredible Rice Pudding, 18

Incredibly Tasty Pizza, 66

Indian Lentils, 67

Indian Lentils Mix, 80

Intense Beet Soup, 111

Intense Tofu And Pineapple Mix, 84

Italian Cauliflower Mix, 93

Italian Veggie Side Dish, 46

L

Lemon Jam, 132

Lentils and Lemon Soup, 78

Lentils Curry, 101

Lentils Dal, 102

Lentils Sandwich, 18

Light Jackfruit Dish, 72

M

Mediterranean Stew, 90

Mexican Black Beans, 34

Mexican Quinoa Dish, 91

Mushroom And Peas Risotto, 42

Mushroom Delight, 93

Mushroom Soup, 112

Mushroom Spread, 63

O

Okra Soup, 104

Orange Cake, 129

P

Peach Cobbler, 126

Pears And Dried Fruits Bowls, 127

Pears And Orange Sauce, 130

Pilaf, 47

Pinto Beans And Tasty Rice, 86

Plums and Apples Surprise, 123

Poached Plums, 128

Potatoes And Spinach Mix, 83

Pudding Cake, 125

Pumpkin Breakfast Delight, 21

Pumpkin Cake, 131

Pumpkin Chili, 76

Pumpkin Chili, 96

Pumpkin Pecan Oatmeal, 25

Pumpkin Pudding, 117

Q

Quinoa And Beans Chili, 83

Quinoa And Veggie Mix, 94

Quinoa and Veggies, 77

Quinoa Chili, 95

R

Ratatouille, 85

Rice Porridge, 23

Rice Pudding, 134

Rich Beans Soup, 66

Rich Chickpeas And Lentils Soup, 99

Rich Jackfruit Dish, 102

Rich Lentils Soup, 82

Rich Sweet Potato Soup, 75

Rich White Bean Soup, 84

Root Vegetable Chili, 97

Rustic Mashed Potatoes, 41

S

Scalloped Potatoes, 39

Seitan Stew, 106

Simple Fruity Breakfast, 19

Simple Potatoes Side Dish, 45

Simple Quinoa and Cranberries Breakfast, 14

Simple Tofu Dish, 69

Slow Cooker Breakfast Oats, 24

Spaghetti Squash Bowls, 77

Spaghetti Squash Bowls, 92

Special Beans Dip, 52

Special Jambalaya, 69

Special Minestrone Soup, 88

Special Potatoes Mix, 48

Special Tea Breakfast, 20

Special Veggie Stew, 79

Spicy Carrot Stew, 107

Spicy Pears, 116

Spinach Dip, 59

Spinach Soup, 87

Split Pea Soup, 87

Squash And Spinach Mix, 43

Squash Chili, 81

Stewed Apples, 130

Stewed Plums, 122

Stewed Rhubarb, 124

Strawberries And Rhubarb Marmalade, 133

Strawberries Jam, 132

Strawberry Cobbler, 115

Strawberry Jam, 121

Strawberry Stew, 128

Summer Black Eyed Peas, 35

Sweet and Spicy Nuts, 53

Sweet Apple And Pears Breakfast, 29

Sweet Peanut Butter Cake, 125

Sweet Potato Soup, 91

Sweet Potatoes Pudding, 133

Sweet Potatoes Side Dish, 40

T

Tasty Apple Crisp, 118

Tasty Black Beans Soup, 75

Tasty Breakfast Buns, 16

Tasty Breakfast Burrito, 26

Tasty Mexican Breakfast, 10

Tasty Onion Dip, 52

Tasty Pear Delight, 120

Tasty Spinach Dip, 49

Textured Sweet Potatoes and Lentils Delight, 65

Thai Veggie Mix, 44

Three Bean Dip, 63

Tofu Appetizer, 57

Tofu Burrito, 10

Tomato Soup, 107

V

Vegan Cashew Spread, 58

Vegan Chickpeas Winter Mix, 80

Vegan Gumbo, 103

Vegan Jambalaya, 85

Vegan Rolls, 55

Vegan Veggie Dip, 56

Veggie Appetizer, 60

Veggie Curry, 73

Veggie Medley, 101

W

White Bean Cassoulet, 72

White Beans Stew, 92

Wild Rice Mix, 41

Wonderful Blueberry Butter, 11

Wonderful Breakfast Idea, 20

Wonderful Corn Chowder, 71

Wonderful Plum Butter, 123

Wonderful Wild Rice, 37

Y

Yam Stew, 88